MODERN WORLD LEADERS

Ali Khamenei

MODERN WORLD LEADERS

MODERN WORLD LEADERS

Ali Khamenei

John Murphy

CHELSEA HOUSE
PUBLISHERS
An imprint of Infobase Publishing

Ali Khamenei

Copyright © 2008 by Infobase Publishing

Chelsea House
An imprint of Infobase Publishing
132 West 31st Street
New York, NY 10001

Library of Congress Cataloging-in-Publication Data
Murphy, John, 1968–
  Ali Khamenei / John Murphy.
    p. cm. — (Modern world leaders)
  Includes bibliographical references and index.
  ISBN-13: 978-0-7910-9517-1 (hardcover)
  ISBN-10: 0-7910-9517-7 (hardcover)
  1. Khamenei, Ali. 2. Presidents—Iran—Biography. 3. Iran—Politics and government—1979–1997. I. Title. II. Series.
  DS318.84.K45M868 2007
  955.05'44092—dc22
  [B]   2007008077

Chelsea House books are available at special discounts when purchased in bulk quantities for businesses, associations, institutions, or sales promotions. Please call our Special Sales Department in New York at (212) 967-8800 or (800) 322-8755.

You can find Chelsea House on the World Wide Web at http://www.chelseahouse.com

Text design by Erik Lindstrom
Cover design by Takeshi Takahashi

Printed in the United States of America

Bang EJB 10 9 8 7 6 5 4 3 2 1

This book is printed on acid-free paper.

All links and Web addresses were checked and verified to be correct at the time of publication. Because of the dynamic nature of the Web, some addresses and links may have changed since publication and may no longer be valid.

TABLE OF CONTENTS

ARTHUR M. SCHLESINGER, JR.

On Leadership

Leadership, it may be said, is really what makes the world go round. Love no doubt smoothes the passage; but love is a private transaction between consenting adults. Leadership is a public transaction with history. The idea of leadership affirms the capacity of individuals to move, inspire, and mobilize masses of people so that they act together in pursuit of an end. Sometimes leadership serves good purposes, sometimes bad; but whether the end is benign or evil, great leaders are those men and women who leave their personal stamp on history.

Now, the very concept of leadership implies the proposition that individuals can make a difference. This proposition has never been universally accepted. From classical times to the present day, eminent thinkers have regarded individuals as no more than the agents and pawns of larger forces, whether the gods and goddesses of the ancient world or, in the modern era, race, class, nation, the dialectic, the will of the people, the spirit of the times, history itself. Against such forces, the individual dwindles into insignificance.

So contends the thesis of historical determinism. Tolstoy's great novel *War and Peace* offers a famous statement of the case. Why, Tolstoy asked, did millions of men in the Napoleonic Wars, denying their human feelings and their common sense, move back and forth across Europe slaughtering their fellows? "The war," Tolstoy answered, "was bound to happen simply because it was bound to happen." All prior history determined it. As for leaders, they, Tolstoy said, "are but the labels that serve to give a name to an end and, like labels, they have the least possible

6

connection with the event." The greater the leader, "the more conspicuous the inevitability and the predestination of every act he commits." The leader, said Tolstoy, is "the slave of history."

Determinism takes many forms. Marxism is the determinism of class. Nazism the determinism of race. But the idea of men and women as the slaves of history runs athwart the deepest human instincts. Rigid determinism abolishes the idea of human freedom—the assumption of free choice that underlies every move we make, every word we speak, every thought we think. It abolishes the idea of human responsibility, since it is manifestly unfair to reward or punish people for actions that are by definition beyond their control. No one can live consistently by any deterministic creed. The Marxist states prove this themselves by their extreme susceptibility to the cult of leadership.

More than that, history refutes the idea that individuals make no difference. In December 1931, a British politician crossing Fifth Avenue in New York City between 76th and 77th streets around 10:30 P.M. looked in the wrong direction and was knocked down by an automobile—a moment, he later recalled, of a man aghast, a world aglare: "I do not understand why I was not broken like an eggshell or squashed like a gooseberry." Fourteen months later an American politician, sitting in an open car in Miami, Florida, was fired on by an assassin; the man beside him was hit. Those who believe that individuals make no difference to history might well ponder whether the next two decades would have been the same had Mario Constasino's car killed Winston Churchill in 1931 and Giuseppe Zangara's bullet killed Franklin Roosevelt in 1933. Suppose, in addition, that Lenin had died of typhus in Siberia in 1895 and that Hitler had been killed on the western front in 1916. What would the twentieth century have looked like now?

For better or for worse, individuals do make a difference. "The notion that a people can run itself and its affairs anonymously," wrote the philosopher William James, "is now well known to be the silliest of absurdities. Mankind does nothing save through initiatives on the part of inventors, great or small, and imitation by the rest of us—these are the sole factors in human progress. Individuals of genius show the way, and set the patterns, which common people then adopt and follow."

Leadership, James suggests, means leadership in thought as well as in action. In the long run, leaders in thought may well make the greater difference to the world. "The ideas of economists and political philosophers, both when they are right and when they are wrong," wrote John Maynard Keynes, "are more powerful than is commonly understood. Indeed the world is ruled by little else. Practical men, who believe themselves to be quite exempt from any intellectual influences, are usually the slaves of some defunct economist. . . . The power of vested interests is vastly exaggerated compared with the gradual encroachment of ideas."

But, as Woodrow Wilson once said, "Those only are leaders of men, in the general eye, who lead in action. . . . It is at their hands that new thought gets its translation into the crude language of deeds." Leaders in thought often invent in solitude and obscurity, leaving to later generations the tasks of imitation. Leaders in action—the leaders portrayed in this series—have to be effective in their own time.

And they cannot be effective by themselves. They must act in response to the rhythms of their age. Their genius must be adapted, in a phrase from William James, "to the receptivities of the moment." Leaders are useless without followers. "There goes the mob," said the French politician, hearing a clamor in the streets. "I am their leader. I must follow them." Great leaders turn the inchoate emotions of the mob to purposes of their own. They seize on the opportunities of their time, the hopes, fears, frustrations, crises, potentialities. They succeed when events have prepared the way for them, when the community is awaiting to be aroused, when they can provide the clarifying and organizing ideas. Leadership completes the circuit between the individual and the mass and thereby alters history.

It may alter history for better or for worse. Leaders have been responsible for the most extravagant follies and most monstrous crimes that have beset suffering humanity. They have also been vital in such gains as humanity has made in individual freedom, religious and racial tolerance, social justice, and respect for human rights.

There is no sure way to tell in advance who is going to lead for good and who for evil. But a glance at the gallery of men and women in MODERN WORLD LEADERS suggests some useful tests.

One test is this: Do leaders lead by force or by persuasion? By command or by consent? Through most of history leadership was exercised by the divine right of authority. The duty of followers was to defer and to obey. "Theirs not to reason why/Theirs but to do and die." On occasion, as with the so-called enlightened despots of the eighteenth century in Europe, absolutist leadership was animated by humane purposes. More often, absolutism nourished the passion for domination, land, gold, and conquest and resulted in tyranny.

The great revolution of modern times has been the revolution of equality. "Perhaps no form of government," wrote the British historian James Bryce in his study of the United States, *The American Commonwealth*, "needs great leaders so much as democracy." The idea that all people should be equal in their legal condition has undermined the old structure of authority, hierarchy, and deference. The revolution of equality has had two contrary effects on the nature of leadership. For equality, as Alexis de Tocqueville pointed out in his great study *Democracy in America*, might mean equality in servitude as well as equality in freedom.

"I know of only two methods of establishing equality in the political world," Tocqueville wrote. "Rights must be given to every citizen, or none at all to anyone . . . save one, who is the master of all." There was no middle ground "between the sovereignty of all and the absolute power of one man." In his astonishing prediction of twentieth-century totalitarian dictatorship, Tocqueville explained how the revolution of equality could lead to the *Führerprinzip* and more terrible absolutism than the world had ever known.

But when rights are given to every citizen and the sovereignty of all is established, the problem of leadership takes a new form, becomes more exacting than ever before. It is easy to issue commands and enforce them by the rope and the stake, the concentration camp and the *gulag*. It is much harder to use argument and achievement to overcome opposition and win consent. The Founding Fathers of the United States understood the difficulty. They believed that history had given them the opportunity to decide, as Alexander Hamilton wrote in the first Federalist Paper, whether men are indeed capable of basing government on "reflection and choice, or whether they are forever destined to depend . . . on accident and force."

Government by reflection and choice called for a new style of leadership and a new quality of followership. It required leaders to be responsive to popular concerns, and it required followers to be active and informed participants in the process. Democracy does not eliminate emotion from politics; sometimes it fosters demagoguery; but it is confident that, as the greatest of democratic leaders put it, you cannot fool all of the people all of the time. It measures leadership by results and retires those who overreach or falter or fail.

It is true that in the long run despots are measured by results too. But they can postpone the day of judgment, sometimes indefinitely, and in the meantime they can do infinite harm. It is also true that democracy is no guarantee of virtue and intelligence in government, for the voice of the people is not necessarily the voice of God. But democracy, by assuring the right of opposition, offers built-in resistance to the evils inherent in absolutism. As the theologian Reinhold Niebuhr summed it up, "Man's capacity for justice makes democracy possible, but man's inclination to justice makes democracy necessary."

A second test for leadership is the end for which power is sought. When leaders have as their goal the supremacy of a master race or the promotion of totalitarian revolution or the acquisition and exploitation of colonies or the protection of greed and privilege or the preservation of personal power, it is likely that their leadership will do little to advance the cause of humanity. When their goal is the abolition of slavery, the liberation of women, the enlargement of opportunity for the poor and powerless, the extension of equal rights to racial minorities, the defense of the freedoms of expression and opposition, it is likely that their leadership will increase the sum of human liberty and welfare.

Leaders have done great harm to the world. They have also conferred great benefits. You will find both sorts in this series. Even "good" leaders must be regarded with a certain wariness. Leaders are not demigods; they put on their trousers one leg after another just like ordinary mortals. No leader is infallible, and every leader needs to be reminded of this at regular intervals. Irreverence irritates leaders but is their salvation. Unquestioning submission corrupts leaders and demeans followers. Making a cult of a leader is always a mistake. Fortunately hero worship generates its own antidote. "Every hero," said Emerson, "becomes a bore at last."

The single benefit the great leaders confer is to embolden the rest of us to live according to our own best selves, to be active, insistent, and resolute in affirming our own sense of things. For great leaders attest to the reality of human freedom against the supposed inevitabilities of history. And they attest to the wisdom and power that may lie within the most unlikely of us, which is why Abraham Lincoln remains the supreme example of great leadership. A great leader, said Emerson, exhibits new possibilities to all humanity. "We feed on genius. . . . Great men exist that there may be greater men."

Great leaders, in short, justify themselves by emancipating and empowering their followers. So humanity struggles to master its destiny, remembering with Alexis de Tocqueville: "It is true that around every man a fatal circle is traced beyond which he cannot pass; but within the wide verge of that circle he is powerful and free; as it is with man, so with communities." ●

Introduction

I t is often assumed that most world leaders are children of privilege who rose to their positions of power by using their family wealth and contacts. Perhaps they influenced the political process and "bought" the support of voters, political patrons, and power brokers. In some cases, they simply inherited the reins of power, which were handed down to them by an older relative. Yet there are also many examples of individuals who seem to come out of nowhere, from humble backgrounds, and somehow manage against all odds to scramble and fight their way to the top. One such individual is the powerful spiritual leader of Iran, Ali Khamenei.

HUMBLE ORIGINS

Sayyed Ali Khamenei, the future ayatollah of Iran, was born into a one-room house in the city of Mashhad. His parents were poor and very religious. His father, Sayyed Javad Khamenei, was a well-respected Muslim scholar, yet he insisted on living in an extremely simple, humble manner. Khamenei remembers many nights in which the family dinner consisted of bread and raisins. Finding enough provisions to create even this basic meal was often difficult.

Encouraged in his religious studies by his beloved father, Ali Khamenei became a serious, hard-working student. He made up in industry and discipline what he lacked in wealth and connections. He began to attend some of the leading Islamic schools and was taught by the greatest and most revered religious scholars of the day.

Ayatollah Ali Khamenei is the supreme leader, otherwise known as the spiritual leader, of Iran. As supreme leader, Khamenei is the final authority on political and governmental matters, superseding the power of Iran's president. Khamenei became Iran's supreme leader in 1989, upon the death of his predecessor, Ayotollah Khomenei.

One of his teachers—and his greatest patron—was the Ayatollah Khomeini, the Islamic fundamentalist and revolutionary leader who led the successful fight to depose the unpopular and dictatorial shah of Iran in 1979. Riding Khomeini's coattails, Khamenei would rise from poverty and obscurity to seize control of one of the world's most proud, influential, and politically volatile nations.

MIRROR IMAGES

Ali Khamenei's dynamic and turbulent personal story is in many ways mirrored by the equally shifting fortunes of Iran throughout its long and eventful history. The story of Khamenei's life is inseparable from the long, turbulent history of Iran. Both are characterized by impoverishment, deprivation, sharp reversals of fortune, brutality, repression, complicated political manipulations, and a rise to global power and influence.

Whether he's regarded as grand ayatollah, Iranian patriot and liberator, or repressive, fanatical religious dictator, however, there is no question that Khamenei has come a long way from the one-room house, meager family dinners, prison, and exile of his youth. He is widely regarded as the most powerful figure within Iran's complex and multilayered governing system. Understanding him is the key to understanding Iran's actions, reactions, and policies, and understanding Khamenei requires an understanding of Iran, its culture, and its history.

The story of Khamenei is the story of Iran. Iran's history and Khamenei's place within it are certain to determine the nation's future actions on the world stage. These actions, in turn, are likely to shape the course of the history of the next century worldwide. As Iran stands on the brink of acquiring the ability to make nuclear weapons, its central importance to the Middle East, to the growing divide between the Western and Islamic worlds, and to the safety and security of the United States is ever greater. It is essential, therefore, to become familiar with the man who is likely to be one of the most important and influential world leaders of the twenty-first century.

1

The History of Persia

THE ADVERSITY, STUBBORNNESS, PERSISTENCE, AND PASSIONATE spirituality that characterizes the life of Ali Khamenei also characterizes the lives of his people and his nation. The Iranians—or Persians, as they are still often called—share a history that is fraught with contradictions, including devastating war and flourishing culture, poverty and riches, invasion and empire, defeat and triumph. The stark contradictions and dramatic turnabouts of Khamenei's own life are mirrored by those of Iran itself.

THE EARLIEST PEOPLES

It is believed that the first people to inhabit present-day Iran— around 3000 B.C.—were hunter-gatherers and nomadic tribes. The land they occupied was hardly welcoming. Iran is surrounded by three daunting mountain ranges, while the heart of the land consists of a vast, arid plateau; deserts; few rivers; and poor soil. More than half of the territory of present-day Iran cannot be cultivated.

Though Iranian mythology points to the nation's first founder as Kiyumars, a wild mountain man who dressed in animal skins, it was not until about 2000 B.C. that a settled society was founded in this forbidding land by the Elamites. They lived in the southwest of modern-day Iran, on the margins of the Sumerian civilization. Sumer was centered in present-day Iraq, and part of its territory is often cited as the location of the biblical Garden of Eden. Part of what enabled the Elamites to create a stable, thriving society—one that included advanced technology and art—in an otherwise inhospitable land was their proximity to the Sumerians.

THE ARRIVAL OF THE ARYANS

The Elamites' flourishing society would prove to be fragile, however, as the first of many future instances of invasion and conquest was acted out in Iran beginning around 1000 B.C. At this time, numerous tribes of Aryans—an Indo-European race of peoples—began to migrate from central Asia and Eastern Europe.

Three of these tribes conquered and settled large regions in Iran. The Scythians gathered around the Black Sea area of the northwest. The Medes came to occupy the vast center of Iran. And the Persians established themselves in the south. Other Aryan tribes continued to migrate westward, eventually settling in northern Europe. These would be the Aryans who would come to be associated with the semilegendary founding race of Germanic and Scandinavian peoples. The word "Iran" means "land of the Aryans," and this was the name given the country in the early twentieth century by the second-to-last shah of Iran, Reza Shah, who objected to the term "Persia" because most Iranians were not, in fact, ethnic Persians.

Though the Persians would eventually become the people most identified with Iran and its period of greatest power and

ZOROASTRIANISM WOULD HAVE FAR-REACHING INFLUENCES, EVEN COMING TO INFORM THE TENETS OF JUDAISM, CHRISTIANITY, AND ISLAM.

achievement, it was another Aryan tribe that initially had the most power. The Medes, thanks in part to geography and circumstances, created a cohesive and unified society. Constantly harried by the Assyrian Empire to the west, the Medes established a stronghold community in the Zagros Mountains. They also developed a sense of common cause and nationhood, forged by almost constant warfare with their far stronger Assyrian neighbors.

ZOROASTRIANISM

The single greatest contribution, not only to Iranian history and culture but to world civilization, during the time of the Medes was the religion known as Zoroastrianism. This innovative faith, believed to be the world's first monotheistic religion (worshipping one god only), would have far-reaching influences, even coming to inform the tenets of Judaism, Christianity, and Islam. It would also forever color the way Iranians thought and felt about justice, good, evil, and righteous leadership, determining in large part which spiritual and political leaders they championed and which they grew disillusioned with. The rise to prominence of both Ayatollah Khomeini and Ali Khamenei can be understood in part through the legacy imparted by Zoroastrianism and the enduring spiritual and political culture it created in Iran.

Zoroastrianism is named after a man named Zoroaster (perhaps better known in the West by the Greek version of his name, Zarathustra). Zoroaster was a seventh-century B.C. preacher who claimed to have received a divine vision concerning good and evil, their effect upon humanity, and the

Seventh-century B.C. Iranian prophet Zoroaster consults two oracles in the above image. Zoroaster believed that there was only one god, as opposed to the widely held belief of the time that there was more than one god. The founder of the Zoroastrianism religion, Zoroaster promoted the idea that there is constant battle between good and evil.

individual's responsibility to fight for good in the world. He believed that earlier societies' tendency to worship many gods was a mistaken splintering of the one God into many different aspects and roles and personalities. While making a pilgrimage across the Iranian plateau, Zoroaster taught his followers and those who would listen that there was only one god, named Ahura Mazda. This god was the creator and was associated with goodness, light, and truth. There was also a destroyer, named Ahriman, who embodies evil, darkness, and death.

Zoroaster believed that humanity—and the universe itself—was engaged in a constant battle between good and evil. All of existence proceeded from the results of this perpetual struggle. He also conceived of a Judgment Day, in which all humans would be judged for their actions during their earthly life. The outcome of the judgment would either condemn one to an eternity in hell or reward one with everlasting life in paradise. It is every individual's responsibility to participate actively in this war against evil through good thoughts and good deeds.

Perhaps most important to Iran's future political life, Zoroastrianism also dictated that rulers must be good and just if they are to continue to enjoy Ahura Mazda's favor and the people's support. Rulers in the time of the Medes and Persians (and beyond) were absolute in their power. These were certainly not democracies. Yet it is also true that their subjects did not believe they owed allegiance to any ruler who seemed to be fighting on the side of evil rather than good. If a ruler stood up for the poor and fought corruption and punished evil-doers, it was believed that the land would thrive, and the people would remain devoted. If, on the other hand, a ruler surrounded himself with nasty characters, misused the nation's wealth, and abused his subjects, the land could expect war, calamity, drought, and famine. Anyone who actively worked towards the removal of an evil leader would in fact be blessed by Ahura Mazda.

In this way, Zoroastrianism imposed a code of ethics on even the highest and most powerful leaders and threatened them with removal for bad behavior. It also instilled the belief in Iranians—persisting even today in many respects—that their leaders must be moral and serve as God's agents for goodness, truth, and justice in the world.

Though born during the high-water mark of the civilization of the Medes, Zoroastrianism would survive that civilization's demise and continue to flourish in successive eras and in different Iranian societies dominated by a different religion. It found particularly fertile soil in the era of the Persian Empire.

CYRUS THE GREAT AND THE BIRTH OF THE PERSIAN EMPIRE

A civilization can survive only so long if under constant siege, and the Medes, weakened by prolonged warfare with the Assyrians, were soon eclipsed by the Persians. The Persians had begun to appear in Iran around 900 B.C.

Perhaps to avoid the constant warfare with the Assyrians under which the Medes were laboring, the Persians settled far south of both groups and were allowed to develop an advanced civilization in relative peace, centered on the Iranian plateau, at Fars. As both the Elamites and the Medes were perpetually engaged in battle with the Assyrians, the Persians had an opportunity to gain strength, land, and leverage in Iran. Eventually, the Elamites were conquered by the Assyrians, who were in turn conquered by the Persians and the Babylonians (an empire centered in modern-day Iraq).

In about 559 B.C., a man named Cyrus II (also known as Cyrus the Great) rose to the throne of Persia and quickly set about conquering and then uniting many of the peoples of Iran, including the Medes and the defeated remnants of the Elamites. Believed to be the son of Cambyses, king of the Persians, and Mandane, daughter of the king of the Medes, Cyrus seemed uniquely positioned to unite disparate tribes and peoples of

Iran, allowing the formation of a larger, more powerful union. An alliance of this sort would expand Persian territory and give the kingdom access to precious water and arable land, not to mention the often vast wealth of foreign kings.

It is believed that the Persians' conquering of the Medes was a relatively smooth and peaceful process, compared to the usual violent standards of empire-building. Cyrus believed that enemy tribes and foreign peoples could be incorporated effectively into the growing Persian Empire if they were treated with respect and consideration. Perhaps following the Zoroastrian dictates for the supreme ruler, Cyrus preferred to persuade his enemies to join the empire rather than force a long and bloody war. He also refused to punish or humiliate the peoples he conquered, and he allowed them to maintain their local traditions, governing systems, and organizational structures. He even allowed the conquered people's militaries to continue more or less in tact and be led by the same officers, though now they would be fighting for rather than against the Persians.

This enlightened approach to conquest and empire-building paid off handsomely for Cyrus. After combining forces with the Medes and Elamites, Cyrus ventured beyond Persia and conquered Parthians and Hyrcanians to the east, the Lydians in present-day Turkey (where Cyrus plundered the treasures of the immeasurably wealthy King Croesus), and the Babylonians.

If the reaction to Cyrus's siege of Babylon among the besieged is any indication, Cyrus was at times greeted as a liberator, as a force of positive change that could sweep aside corrupt rulers. Babylonians, disgusted with the misrule of their king, Nabonidus, were said to have opened the gates of the city to Cyrus and invited him in. As he entered, they threw fragrant leaves in his path to honor him and carpet his footfalls. Demonstrating his characteristic respect for local customs and his ability to unite different peoples in a seamless whole, he paid his respects to the Babylonian gods and adopted the traditional titles of Babylonian kingship.

Under Cyrus and his son, Cambyses, who succeeded Cyrus after his death in battle with the nomadic Massagetaes in the northeast corner of Iran in 530 B.C., the Persian Empire extended from Egypt to Greece, from Africa to China, and included modern-day Afghanistan, Pakistan, Iraq, and large swaths of Asia Minor. This massive empire—numbering about 50 million people and larger than those of the Assyrians, Egyptians, and Babylonians before it—was the first of three great Persian empires and is often referred to as the Achaemenid Empire.

DARIUS AND THE TWILIGHT OF THE ACHAEMENIDS

Cambyses' son, Darius, inherited the imperial throne in 522 B.C., and for many years he extended the empire's borders even farther and enhanced its prestige. As the empire grew, it became more difficult to rule in a centrally organized, efficient way.

So Darius created an improved communications system by paving thousands of miles of roads and creating a horse-driven postal system. He created a system of local governorships to establish stable and consistent imperial government and a system of laws throughout the empire. He standardized weights and measures and created a common currency. Also, perhaps in emulation of his grandfather Cyrus, who had built a capital city named Pasargadae ("the dwelling of the Persians") on a lonely plain in Fars, Darius built a new imperial capital at Persepolis. In an even more meaningful nod to Cyrus, Darius ordered that the design of Persepolis incorporate the architectural styles of all of the conquered peoples who had joined the Persian Empire, including Indians, Syrians, Babylonians, Egyptians, Ethiopians, and Libyans.

The construction of Persepolis was meant to celebrate Darius's expansion of the Persian Empire, following his conquests of North Africa, the lower Danube area, the Macedonians, and the Greeks of Thrace. It would be a living monument to both his military successes and, far more important, his status as a supreme ruler, or king of kings. Persepolis stood as a testament to his just kingship, to his fulfillment of the Zoroastrian requirement to be a ruler who unites all people—regardless of race, tribe, or nationality—and protects them from evil. Yet within only a few years of its construction, the seeds of Persepolis's destruction—and that of the entire Achaemenid Empire—would be planted.

In 490 B.C., Darius launched an ill-fated invasion of Greece, resulting in the defeat of the Persians at Marathon by Athenian forces. The supreme ruler's reach may finally have exceeded his grasp. Perhaps in an effort to avenge his father and reassert Persian power, Darius's son Xerxes again invaded Greece in 480 B.C. Initially, things seemed to go well. Leading a Persian army of 200,000 men, Xerxes defeated a spirited but doomed Spartan army of only 300 men at Thermopylae and went on to sack Athens, attacking the Acropolis and burning the Parthenon. The Spartans' brave stand against the Persians at Thermopylae, however, inspired many of the Greek city-states—which often warred amongst themselves—to band together and turn back Xerxes' invasion.

At this point, the tide began to turn against the Persians. Their navy was soon defeated at Salamis by the Athenian fleet. As a result, due to a lack of naval support following the battle of Salamis, the Persians were defeated at Plataea by an army of mixed Greek soldiers led by the Spartans. Any hope of drawing Greece into the fold of the Persian Empire through force or persuasion was dashed forever. Greece would remain forever outside the Persian orbit.

In fact, the tide would turn so completely against the Achaemenid Empire that in 332 B.C., more than 130 years after the death of Xerxes, the Greeks would exact retribution and invade and conquer Persia. Alexander of Macedonia, known to history as Alexander the Great, launched an attack on the

Darius the Great, son of Cambyses, became the king of Persia in 522 B.C. Darius was responsible for expanding the Persian Empire, revising the legal system, improving the infrastructure by paving thousands of miles of roads, and building the short-lived capital city of Persepolis. Darius the Great is pictured above in this detail from an ancient relief.

world's greatest empire with a force of 35,000 men. The final Achaemenid king, Darius III, tried to avoid bloodshed by offering territory to Alexander. The Greek conqueror preferred battle to negotiation and soon set Darius III to flight, leaving the Persian forces in disarray. Alexander conquered the Persian

Empire, eventually reaching as far as Afghanistan and India. He also seized the symbolic throne of Persia—Persepolis—and burned it to the ground.

Alexander was not only interested in vengeance and conquest. He genuinely wished to govern Persia and incorporate its peoples, traditions, and systems within his own growing Greek empire. Yet Alexander died of a fever before this process could be completed, and no worthy successor emerged to hold the empire together. Instead, it was carved up among a number of Greek generals. Persia was ruled by Seleucis, and some Greek influences began to creep into Persian culture. Persian identity and political will, however, remained stubborn and strong, despite the imposition of the Greek language, Greek laws, Greek art, and Greek political culture. A Greek presence in Persia was to remain short-lived.

THE PARTHIAN ERA

In one of history's curious full-circle moments, Persian autonomy was restored by a nomadic tribe of central Asian Aryans very much like the Scythians (from whom they were descended), Medes, and Persians of centuries before. Around the time of Alexander's death in 323 B.C., the Parthians began to migrate from the eastern edge of the Caspian Sea and settle in Iran. They quickly began to assimilate Persian cultures and traditions, and then began to spread into Iran's interior. By the middle of the second century B.C., the Parthians had gained control of most of Persia and vanquished the Seleucid Greeks.

The Parthian Empire would eventually stretch from present-day Armenia to central Asia to the Arabian Sea. The extensive system of roads built in the Achaemenid era was maintained and expanded, allowing for trade with India, China, and the emerging Roman Empire, with whom the Parthians increasingly waged war to protect the integrity of their borders. Having had one brush with Western domination, the Persians were determined to maintain their

THIS DISTRUST OF AND HOSTILITY TO THE WESTERN WORLD WOULD PERSIST TO THE TIME OF ALI KHAMENEI AND BEYOND.

autonomy and identity in the face of a new, expanding, and ambitious Western imperial force. This distrust of and hostility to the Western world would persist to the time of Ali Khamenei and beyond. Indeed, Ali Khamenei's rise to power is in many ways predicated upon suspicion of and anger towards the Western world.

Despite this nationalistic determination and cultural pride, however, no Parthian leader emerged who could effectively unify Persia. Tribal squabbling and all-out warfare broke out, and by A.D. 208, the son of a Zoroastrian shrine-keeper and tribal monarch emerged in the ancient Achaemenid royal city of Fars to assume kingship and reunify Persia. His name was Ardeshir, and within about 15 years he defeated the last of the Parthian rulers and claimed the old Zoroastrian title "shahanshah"—king of kings—from which the title "shah" is derived. The third and final great Persian Empire was born—the Sassanian Empire.

THE SASSANIAN ERA

The Sassanian Empire is characterized by contradictory spiritual revival and religious intolerance; cultural flowering and repressive social control; military might and a gradual erosion of power. Under Ardeshir, the old Zoroastrian traditions were revived, and he and his successors insisted upon their divine right to rule the people. In order to further legitimize their political position, Sassanian rulers both protected and controlled the Zoroastrian priests—known as *magi*—who had been mostly independently operating up to this time. The priests' sacred texts and teachings were used and manipulated to reinforce the supreme ruler's authority and immunity from dissent (disagreement) and rebellion.

Perhaps in reaction to the near-constant military threats of Rome, the emerging Byzantine Empire (the eastern part of the former Roman Empire), and rebellious tribes within Persia, Sassanian rulers tried to exert domestic control by forging a rigidly structured, hierarchical, class-based society. The supreme ruler was on top, followed by magi, judges, and temple keepers. These were followed by the military class. Next came the "professional class" of the royal court—scribes, doctors, poets, astronomers, and accountants. The lowest class was composed of craftspeople, farmers, nomadic herders, merchants, and traders. There was little or no mixing between the classes, and marriages between members of different classes were forbidden. The lower classes were not even allowed to buy property.

Sandra Mackey, author of *The Iranians: Persia, Islam, and the Soul of a Nation*, argues that this institutional elitism imposed by the Sassanians became a hallmark of Iranian society ever after and ultimately gave rise to the kind of revolutionary fervor expressed by Ayatollah Khomeini and Ali Khamenei and embodied by so many Iranians marching and protesting in the streets of Tehran before and after the last shah's fall from power. She writes that this Sassanian attempt at social control "was the beginning of the social-political behavior for centuries. Still existing in a modified form populated by different families at the time of the Muhammad Reza Shah [the last shah of Iran], the call to level this hierarchical system was one of the most forceful elements in the Iranian Revolution of 1979."

Yet, in the years following the 1979 Iranian revolution that deposed the shah, many Iranians came to feel that the supreme leader and his fellow ayatollahs had established an equally rigid hierarchy of power, in cooperation with the business elite and backed by the military and judiciary, leaving the nation's peasants and urban poor thoroughly dominated and demoralized. These cycles of Iranian history often seem impossible to break.

Persian leader Ardashir I ruled during the Sassanian Empire, a period of time characterized by religious revival. Ardashir I established Zoroastrianism as the official religion of the empire. The ruler is depicted in the above relief.

HERESIES, REPRESSION, AND CULTURAL FLOURISHING

Another Sassanian tendency that would become a hallmark of later Iranian society—under the shahs and the post-revolutionary religious clerics like Khomeini and Ali Khamenei—was an intolerance for dissenting religious and political thought. In both the Achaemenian and Parthian eras, local traditions and beliefs were accommodated and absorbed within the dominant Zoroastrian-based Persian culture. The rulers tended to believe that the empire was strengthened by the religious and cultural contributions of its many and various members. During the Sassanian era, however, a number of religious movements arose that were perceived as threats to the political-religious state that the Sassanian Empire had become.

The chief of these "heresies" were Manichaeism (established in the third century A.D. by the religious visionary Mani) and Mazdakism (established in the late fifth century A.D. by the visionary Mazdak). Both religions borrowed heavily from Zoroastrianism, as well as pre-Zoroastrian pagan Iranian beliefs, Christianity, and Buddhism. Both movements gained many followers and began to threaten the power and authority of the Zoroastrian priest class. Furthermore, Mazdakism taught that goodness, peace, and love could only flourish in a society in which everyone was equal and in which a class system did not create envy, resentment, or conflict.

These teachings were profoundly threatening to both the priestly class and the king, and harsh responses were prepared. The Zoroastrian priests, now thoroughly corrupted by power, wealth, and status, ordered both Mani and Mazdak to be killed. Zoroastrian priests were also known to persecute Iranian Jews and Christians, and members of minority religious groups were often forced to pay extremely high taxes.

Despite this tight social control and religious and political repression, however, the Sassanian era represented one of the high points of Persian cultural expression. Much of the iconic art and artifacts associated with the glory of the Persian Empire emerged in the Sassanian era, including opulent palaces, domes, vaults, Persian carpets, painted miniatures, court poetry, and manuals of good government and proper princely conduct and rule.

BYZANTINE DOMINANCE

Flush both with a sense of tightly controlled power and an abundance of wealth and glory, the Sassanians tried to expand their empire's territory and impose its authority upon the Western world. Rather than merely holding the Byzantine Empire at bay, the Sassanians chose to take a more aggressive tack. They would invade Byzantium and attempt to subdue it.

Once again, Persia's contact with the Western world would lead to devastating consequences. The invasion began well in A.D. 602. Within 18 years, the Sassanians had seized control of Antioch, Jerusalem, Sardis, Ephesus, Alexandria, and Egypt. They did not, however, drive the Byzantines from their stronghold of Constantinople (modern-day Istanbul). From this headquarters, Byzantine forces were able to regroup. In 626, they marched north, sailed across the Black Sea, establishing themselves in the Caucuses—the border between Europe and Asia—between modern-day Turkey, Iran, Russia, the Black Sea, and the Caspian Sea.

From the Caucuses, the Byzantines penetrated deep into Persia, not stopping until they reached the Sassanian seat of power, Ctesiphon, in Mesopotamia, just south of present-day Baghdad. The Sassanian king fled, the army fell apart, and the empire itself collapsed within only a few years. The end came when Sassanian generals did the unthinkable; they rose up and assassinated their shahanshah, their king of kings, no doubt arguing that given the war and turmoil that had come to grip Persia, the king had proven himself an agent of diabolic evil, not divine good. A similar spiritual justification would be presented by Khomeini, Ali Khamenei, and other revolutionary clerics in the waning days of the last shah's rule.

With this profoundly daring and outrageous upholding of the uncompromising Zoroastrian code of social conduct, the Persian world came to a sudden end. After years of debilitating warfare with the Byzantines, the Persians had left themselves vulnerable to yet another invasion by a more powerful force relentlessly sweeping across the Iranian plateau. This invasion and conquest, however, would change the very nature, foundation, and fiber of Persian culture in a way that no other foreign occupier had been able to do in the past.

CHAPTER

2

The Islamic Invasion

IN A.D. 610, THE PROPHET MUHAMMAD, A FORMER CAMEL DRIVER SICKENED by the sin and corruption of society, wandered from the city of Mecca into the Arabian desert to meditate. Once there, he received a divine message from the angel Gabriel, urging him to preach to his fellow Arabs about the one true god, Allah.

Muhammad's belief system included divine judgment of the good and wicked, an eternal afterlife in either heaven or hell, the importance of spiritual riches over earthly treasure, the moral requirement to share all wealth, and the equality of all men. These doctrines began to attract many followers, especially among the Arab poor. For this reason, Muhammad and his teachings began to be perceived as a threat to the ruling elite of Mecca. In 622, Muhammad and his followers were forced to flee Mecca for Medina, about 200 miles to the north. This journey is regarded as the birth of Islam, and it is recreated every year by devout Muslim pilgrims.

Within a year of Muhammad's death, the entire Arabian peninsula was converted to Islam.

Eight years later, Muhammad and a thousand followers returned to Mecca, seized power, and converted the city to Islam. By the time of his death in 632, Muhammad was no longer a humble desert visionary. He now claimed to be the last of a long line of Old Testament prophets who tried to turn people's attention to the one true god. He even believed that Jesus, said to be the son of God by Christians, was merely another prophet, like himself. There was no shortage of believers in his message. Within a year of Muhammad's death, the entire Arabian peninsula was converted to Islam.

PERSIA'S CONVERSION TO ISLAM

Islam's influence would not be confined to Arabia, however. The tenets of Islam required preaching to and conversion of infidels, or unbelievers, by force if necessary. This missionary impulse, coupled with the more earthly human desire to gain more power, territory, and wealth, inspired Muslim soldiers to fan out from the Arabian peninsula and conquer Syria and Byzantium. Only 10 years after the Prophet's death, Persia would be the next to fall to the forces of Allah.

The end came quickly for Sassanian Persia. Exhausted and demoralized by their long years of war with Byzantium, the Persian soldiers were no match for an Arab force that was fired by religion and intent upon plundering the riches of the Persian Empire. The first military engagement occurred in 637 at Qadisiya, resulting in the death of the Persian commander and a chaotic Persian retreat. One year later, the Sassanian seat of power—the opulent palace at Ctesiphon—fell to the Arabs. The Persian defeat at Nihavand in 642 allowed Arab forces to

Muhammad *(above)* was the founder of Islam and is believed by many to have been a prophet. Muhammad gained a following with his teachings and became a threat to the ruling elite, which forced him to flee to Medina. The trip is regarded as the birth of Islam, and every year Muslims make a pilgrimage to mark the beginning of the Islamic calendar.

ISLAM TAUGHT EQUALITY OF ALL MEN AND INSISTED THAT ONE'S ALLEGIANCE AND LOYALTY BELONGED TO ALLAH, NOT TO ANY STATE OR LEADER.

pour into the Iranian plateau and enter the region of Fars. At the city of Istakhr in Fars, the Persian forces mounted a doomed last stand. By 651, Persia was an Arab-ruled state.

The effort to convert Persians to Islam began immediately but proved to be a long, drawn-out process. It is believed that it took until the ninth century for a majority of Iranians to be converted to Islam. In many respects, it was not a great leap for Persians to make between Zoroastrianism and Islam. Both religions saw a cosmic struggle between good and evil as central to human existence. Both religions demanded faith in only one "true" god. Both were preoccupied with notions of truth and justice, heaven and hell.

Yet Persians were also preoccupied with "Persianness," with a sense of their glorious history and divinely directed destiny as a nation and as a people. Related to this was their faith in the king of kings, a living representative of God on earth, who was just, all-powerful, and, as long as he fought for good, deserving of absolute loyalty and obedience. They were justly proud of their culture and all they had been able to achieve and felt somewhat superior to their Arab conquerors. Though Arabs were the chosen people of Allah, they were considered by "cultured" Persians to be mere desert-dwelling, animal-herding barbarians.

Islam taught equality of all men and insisted that one's allegiance and loyalty belonged to Allah, not to any state or leader. Because all believers were equal, there could be no king, and because Allah was supreme over all, demanding and deserving of one's total devotion, kingdoms and states and national borders were irrelevant. Allah's heavenly kingdom should be the believer's focus and desire; identification with and commitment to earthly societies was debased.

This devaluing of all that Persians held most dear about themselves, their society, their culture, and their history made the Arab brand of Islam an awkward match for many. This religious and cultural divide would only get wider as disputes broke out within the Islamic world over who was the rightful successor to Muhammad's leadership and ministry.

THE SHIITE-SUNNI SPLIT

The Prophet Muhammad died without appointing his successor. Arabian tribal traditions usually determined leadership questions by choosing a replacement among the deceased leader's descendants and relatives or by choosing a new leader (who may or may not have been related to the deceased leader) through tribal consensus (general agreement). Muhammad had no son, so attention fell upon two main candidates for succession—Ali, the Prophet's cousin and son-in-law (he was married to Muhammad's daughter), and Abu Bakr, Muhammad's father-in-law and longtime companion and adviser.

A majority of the original companions of Muhammad selected Abu Bakr as *caliph* (or successor to Muhammad), but a significant number were committed to Ali, believing leadership should pass down along the Prophet's bloodlines. Ali lived in a simple, humble style, much like that of Muhammad himself. This stood in stark contrast to the wealthy leaders of Mecca who seemed far more interested in riches and luxury than matters of the spirit. For this reason, Ali, though an Arab, attracted much support from non-Arab Muslims, such as the Persians. They responded not only to his outsider status within Islam, but also to his message of simple truth and justice and his criticism of the Arab elites.

Ali eventually did become the caliph in 656, but he was assassinated in 661. His death provoked a new succession crisis.

Ali's supporters argued that his sons should become caliphs, thereby preserving succession through the Prophet's bloodline. The ruling Mecca elite, however, preferred Mu'awiya, of the influential Umayyads. Ali's sons, perhaps sensing that there could be no fighting the power of the Mecca aristocracy, withdrew their claims, and Mu'awiya became caliph. Yet Ali's followers did not abandon their belief in the hereditary succession of the caliphate, and they formed their own party in opposition to the Umayyads and their Mecca backers. The party was called "Shi'at Ali," or the Party of Ali. It became popularly known as Shi'ah, and its supporters as Shiites.

When Mu'awiya died in 680, one of Ali's sons, Hussein, attempted to seize the caliphate from Mu'awiya's successor, his son Yazid. Hussein, his brother Abbas, and more than 70 followers were killed in battle at Karbala, a day that has become the holiest day in the Shiite religious calendar. Ali and Hussein are greatly revered to this day by Shiite Muslims. They are honored and celebrated for their insistence on maintaining the purity of the Islamic faith, their passionate commitment to justice, and their rebuke—through their words and example—to the high-living corruption and worldly luxury of the Mecca religious establishment. Indeed, Ali is believed by Shiites to be the single most just, brave, and virtuous human being ever to have lived, other than the Prophet Muhammad himself.

Though a majority in Iran and Iraq, Shiites represent a minority of Muslims. The great majority of Muslims are Sunni, spiritual descendants of the Arab Mecca establishment who seized control of the caliphate. These two Islamic sects began to develop independently of each other. Very broadly, they can be said to divide along ethnic lines, with non-Arab Persians tending to be Shiite and Arab Muslims tending to be Sunni. This is something of an oversimplification, however, and there are many exceptions to the rule.

Shiite Muslims believe that imams, or leaders appointed by God, use their divine insight to guide their people. According to Shiite Muslims, there are only twelve imams who are direct descendents of the Prophet. In the above ancient Persian image, the Prophet is pictured with his imams.

SHIITE RELIGIOUS AND EDUCATIONAL STRUCTURES

One of the results of this split in Islam was that each sect developed different doctrines and organized its religious hierarchy quite differently. In a very general sense, the split can be seen as akin to that of the Protestant and Catholic branches of Christianity. Just as Protestants felt that God's word was accurately recorded and preserved in the Bible and was available to all seekers without the interpretive help of priests serving as mediators between God and humans, Sunni Muslims believe that the Koran and the words of the Prophet contain all truth, and nothing more is needed. Other than the texts that contain the earliest interpretations of the Koran and the Prophet's teachings, no further interpretive guidance is required from religious leaders. Therefore, as in many Protestant churches, the religious hierarchy is fairly simple and streamlined, and the faithful take much personal responsibility for their spiritual education and health.

Shiite Muslims, on the other hand, believe that imams are divinely inspired, that they receive guidance and wisdom directly from God, and, in turn, use this insight to guide their people in their spiritual and earthly lives. Shiites believe that there have been only 12 true imams, all descended directly from the Prophet. These include Ali and his sons Hussein and Hasan. The twelfth imam was said to have been hidden away when still a baby to protect his life against Sunni enemies bent on assassinating him. While in hiding, he was said to have entered a sort of state of spiritual suspended animation. It is believed he will return again to usher in a period of justice in advance of a Day of Judgment.

In this suspended state, Shiites are left without a divinely inspired imam to teach and guide them. Therefore, earthly representatives must be appointed to serve as a proxy twelfth imam. These men are referred to as *mujtahids*, and they are granted the power to interpret the sacred texts of the Koran and the Prophet. This power is known as *ijtihad*. The most respected mujtahids were known by the title *marja-e taqlid*, which means "source of emulation." In this role, a marja-e taqlid serves as a role model for his people, teaching them through word and deed how to live their lives properly, in accordance with God's wishes and the principles of the Koran and the Prophet. The marja-e taqlid who is seen as the most pure, just, and righteous is called a *marja-e taqlid al-mutlaq*, a supreme or absolute marja-e taqlid.

As this complex hierarchy of religious leaders formed, the process of religious education and advancement also became more elaborate and involved. Anyone wishing to become a cleric, or *mullah*, first attended a seminary, or *madrassa*. Two of the most important and respected Shiite seminaries are Qom in Iran and Najaf in Iraq, both of which Ali Khamenei attended in his youth. Upon graduation, the clerics would either teach in villages or remain in the seminary to teach, while being supervised by higher-ranking clerics.

If, in his role as teacher and spiritual guide to his pupils and congregations, the young cleric demonstrated a thorough familiarity with and knowledge of the scriptures and showed genuine spiritual insights, he would be given the title *hojjat-ol Islam* (which means "proof of Islam"). Clerics who continue to prove their exceptional knowledge of scripture and pure embodiment of Islamic principles receive the title *ayatollah* (meaning "sign of God"). To receive this distinction, they must write a lengthy thesis (a book-length research paper) on the subject of how people should live their daily lives in accordance with the teachings of the Koran and the Prophet. The pinnacle of earthly and spiritual attainment for a Shiite cleric is the title *ayatollah al-uzma*, ("Grand Ayatollah," or "greatest sign of God").

This is exactly the educational and spiritual path followed by Ali Khamenei and his mentor, Ayatollah Khomeini. In the twentieth century, Grand Ayatollah Khomeini, and to a lesser extent Ali Khamenei, would inherit the high regard Iranians traditionally extended to their "king of kings," the shahs. Like the Zoroastrian kings who were believed to be the earthly representatives of the god Ahura Mazda, modern-day Iranian religious leaders were looked to as figures of truth, justice, purity, and goodness. Expected to be both charismatic and existing somewhat above and apart from ordinary earthly life, powerful clerics like Khomeini and Ali Khamenei would "speak truth to power," railing against the abuses and corruption of tyrannical secular leaders (most notably the last shah of Iran). They would also spearhead an Islamic revolution that would depose a leader deemed to be working for the forces of evil and reestablish a divinely ruled and guided Iran.

THE ABBASID DYNASTY AND PERSIAN CULTURAL DOMINANCE

In the years following Hussein's defeat at Karbala in 680, the Islamic Empire, ruled by the Umayyads, began to sink under its own corrupt weight. Umayyad caliphs were far more interested in their own pleasure and wealth than in matters of the spirit, and they served as very poor role models for the people they were expected to guide and teach. Some of them even openly mocked the Prophet and his commitment to poverty and humility.

The Umayyad dynasty also continued to insist that Islam was an Arab religion, and they treated non-Arab Muslims as second-class citizens. Iran was made to feel neglected, like it existed on the forgotten margins of the empire, insignificant and beneath the notice of the elites of Mecca and Damascus. Many Muslims, Arab and non-Arab, Sunni and Shiite, began to chafe under this debased, immoral leadership.

Tensions came to a head in 750 when supporters of the Abbasids, a clan claiming direct descent from the Prophet, roundly defeated 12,000 Umayyad troops in what is now Iraq. They were led by Abu Muslim, a former slave who railed against the corruption of the Umayyad caliphs. The fourteenth

Umayyad caliph fled to Egypt, where he was found hiding in a Christian church and decapitated.

With the emergence and rise of the Abbasid dynasty, Islam and the Islamic empire were opened up to Persian cultural and spiritual influences, and Arab domination of the religion and society was broken. The empire's capital shifted from Damascus, in modern-day Syria, to Baghdad, in modern-day Iraq. The old Persian postal and road systems were revived, and Iran again became a crossroads of world trade and a marketplace of ideas and influences. Looking back to the glory days of the Persian Empire and the Sassanian era in particular, Persian intellectual, artistic, architectural, literary, stylistic, and spiritual influences began to infuse Islam. This resulted in a cultural and technological high-water mark for the Islamic world, as the famously open-minded Persians embraced Greek and Indian scientific learning, philosophy, theology, and mathematics.

The Persian language was also revived, and, though now dappled with Arabic words, still expressed a worldview and spirituality that was as distinctively Persian—mystical, mythological, historical, action-packed, densely layered—as it was Islamic. This golden age of Persian literature also served as an overt rebuke to what Persians often believed was an inferior, crude, barbaric Arab culture. The most important work of this period, aside from the famous *One Thousand and One Nights* (which introduced the world to Aladdin, Ali Baba, and Sinbad), is the poet Ferdowsi's tenth-century epic *Shanameh* ("The Book of Kings"), a 60,000-line poem recounting the thousand years of Persian history stretching from the Achaemenian to the Sassanian eras. The balance of power had shifted, and the Persians were now in a position to look upon their former Arab masters with contempt, despite their shared religion and its continued domination by Arab caliphs.

Within a few decades of the completion of Ferdowsi's *Shanameh* and its stirring tribute to the glories of Persian

> ## THOUGH SHOCKINGLY VIOLENT, KHAN WAS ALSO A BRILLIANT MILITARY TACTICIAN, TERRORIZING, SACKING, AND SUBDUING MOST OF CENTRAL ASIA AND THE FORMER PERSIAN EMPIRE WITHIN ONLY A FEW YEARS.

kingship, however, Persian supremacy would once again be toppled and humbled.

TURKIC, MONGOL, AND TATAR INVASIONS

Weakened by civil war and a splintering into local dynastic rule, Iran once again became vulnerable to invaders. This time it was Seljuk Turks who emerged from central Asia early in the eleventh century. Devotees of Sunni Islam, they eventually gained control of Iran and vanquished the various local Shiite dynasties.

Yet, within a hundred years, the Turks, too, were forced to yield to an invading force—the much dreaded and terrifying Mongols, also of central Asia, led by the savage and bloodthirsty Genghis Khan. Though shockingly violent, Khan was also a brilliant military tactician, terrorizing, sacking, and subduing most of central Asia and the former Persian Empire within only a few years. Contemporary accounts suggest that nearly every Persian city, town, and village fell victim to the Mongols' slaughter.

As pagans, the Mongols had no respect for Islam and went out of their way to desecrate and destroy holy sites, mosques, and sacred texts. In the various waves of Mongol and Tatar (another central Asian tribe) attacks that occurred between 1217 and 1405, many millions of Iranians were murdered, their bodies mutilated, and their skulls often piled up in towering pyramids. Many others were enslaved. It would take until the mid-twentieth century before Iran's population returned to pre-Mongol invasion numbers. These nomadic Asian warrior-peoples were less interested in empire building and more interested in extracting the wealth of the conquered territories, including herds and foraging land. The once-glorious Persian Empire had become a mere Mongol territory, razed, ravaged, and impoverished.

SUFISM AND THE SAFAVID DYNASTY

Perhaps all history is cyclical, but no nation's history seems more so than Iran's. In the wake of the Turk, Mongol, and Tatar invasions and massacres, Iran would rise again from its ashes and spawn a homegrown dynasty. Once again, this new political and dynastic movement was inspired and sustained by religion. In the seventh century, an offshoot of Shi'ah Islam emerged in the Muslim world. It was known as Sufism, a sect of mystical believers who distrusted the worldly power, authority, and corruption of Islamic clerics and the elaborate laws and scriptural interpretations that had encrusted the religion. They believed that the Koran and the Prophet's insistence on forming a union with the one true god was best achieved not with the help of clerics, complicated church hierarchies, or complex religious writings, but through separation from the world, meditation, and mystical exercises, such as singing, praying, and dancing. These activities were all designed to inspire a state of ecstasy.

One group of Sufis evolved from a group of monk-like brothers into a military organization bent on holy war against unbelievers. Initially, this group, the Safavids, did battle with Christians in the Caucuses region. But, in 1501, under the leadership of a young man named Ismail, the Safavids, who were Turkoman tribesmen from northern Iran, began to establish a dynasty that controlled all of Iran (extending also to Baghdad and eastern Turkey) for the next two centuries.

Creating stability and unity, by force when necessary, Ismail brought to an end Iran's long period of civil war, invasion,

Shah Ismail was the leader of the Safavid dynasty that ruled over the Iranian empire for two centuries. Shah Ismail brought stability to the war-torn Iranian land, and declared Shi'ah Islam as the official religion of the empire. In the portrait above, Shah Ismail battles the Uzbek Shibani Khan.

bloodshed, and slaughter. He also made Shi'ah Islam the official religion of Iran, forcing Sunni Muslims to flee and anger-
ing the Ottoman Turk empire, a Sunni state, across the border.
The Ottoman Empire was the world's single greatest Islamic

power in the sixteenth century. Ismail declared that all Sunni religious practices must cease, and he ordered decapitated anyone caught practicing that version of the faith. He invited Shiite clerics from Lebanon to come and take over Sunni mosques, and public rallies in which Sunni Islam was violently cursed were held.

Having established his empire and restored Persian pride and identity, Ismail faded away in surprising fashion. After suffering a relatively minor defeat in battle against the Ottomans in 1514, Ismail seemed to go into mourning and surrendered to drunkenness and idle living. He died at the age of 36.

SHAH ABBAS I

The Safavid dynasty remained strong, however, especially under the leadership of Shah Abbas I, the Safavids' greatest leader, who was born in Afghanistan and whose rule was centered in Khorasan, Ali Khamenei's home province. Rising to power at the age of 16, Abbas looked back to Sassanian notions of kingship and set himself up as a king of kings. Just as the shahs of old relied on Zoroastrian priests to support their rule and convince the people of their divine right to govern, Abbas harnessed the influence of Shiite clerics to bolster his stature. He founded many madrassas and gathered Shiite clerics from across the Islamic world to his kingdom. He dressed and lived simply, forging connections to "common people." He went on long pilgrimages.

All of this cast Abbas as the just ruler in the eyes of his subjects. Abbas had restored the close cooperation of church and state. He reestablished the Sassanian model of a ruler who derives his power from the ranks of the clerics, and clerics who enjoy the patronage and prestige that can be granted only by a king. This same dynamic, in slightly different form, is what allowed both Ayatollah Khomeini and Ali Khamenei to rise to power and maintain their tight hold on it and on their people.

Yet the wheel of fortune would turn once again for Iran. In 1722, tribesmen from Afghanistan invaded and conquered much of Iran, bringing the Safavid dynasty to an end. Within 70 years, however, the political scene would change once again. Another Turkic tribe originally from central Asia, the Qajars, who had lived in Iran since the fourteenth century, rose to dominance. They would clumsily usher Iran into the modern world and oversee a period of bewildering global change, instability, and power plays. Long subject to the invasions of neighboring tribes and empires, Iran was about to become the pawn of industrialized Western powers.

3

The History of Modern Iran

IN THE NINETEENTH CENTURY, BRITAIN AND RUSSIA WERE ENGAGED IN WHAT became known as the Great Game. The world's two greatest powers were competing furiously for influence over the nations of Asia and access to their natural resources and other wealth. Iran, having suffered a humiliating defeat to Russia in Georgia and the Caucuses region in the early years of the nineteenth century, was forced to roll back its border.

Sensing an opportunity for revenge made possible by the British-Russian rivalry, the shah at the time signed a treaty with the British, granting them the right to station troops in Iran in exchange for protection and military training. Britain was interested in countering Russian influence in the region and in using Iran as a buffer between the Russians and Britain's prized colony of India.

This agreement with the British, known as the Definitive Treaty of 1814, opened a long period in which Iran tried to play

OUTRAGED MERCHANTS, FARMERS, AND CLERICS BANDED TOGETHER TO PROTEST THE TOBACCO DEAL AND THE QAJAR REGIME'S GENERAL SELLING OUT OF THE NATION'S INTEREST FOR ITS OWN PERSONAL ENRICHMENT.

world powers against each other in order to gain power, stature, and wealth. Generally speaking, the effort failed, and Iran was simply used and abused as the world powers, including the United States, shifted their spheres of influence and raided the nation of its wealth and resources. As the Western world grew richer and more industrialized, Iran seemed to wither on the vine. Its roads were neglected, its communication systems were antiquated, poor land use led to desertification, and its traditional trade dried up once Western manufactured goods entered the global marketplace.

CORRUPTION AND OUTRAGE

A further strain was provided by the shahs themselves, who indulged in debt spending and lavish lifestyles as the people sank into desperate poverty. The shahs became so desperate for cash that they began to sign trade treaties that offered representatives of foreign nations—particularly Britain—exclusive rights to Iran's natural resources and to the manufacturing and selling of goods in Iran. In 1891, for example, the shah offered a British citizen a monopoly on all tobacco sold in Iran, including on tobacco that was grown in Iran. The nation's economy and trade became, to a large extent, controlled by foreigners.

Outraged merchants, farmers, and clerics banded together to protest the tobacco deal and the Qajar regime's general selling out of the nation's interest for its own personal enrichment. This revolt led to the repeal of the deal. Yet the Qajars didn't learn their lesson. Within 10 years, Iran agreed to import

The shah of Persia, Nasser-Al-Din, is seen with Prince Leopold, Duke of Albany, in this 1880 photograph. In 1890, the shah signed a contract with a British man, giving him ownership of the Iranian tobacco industry. The contract was later canceled.

Russian goods at low tariffs (thereby undercutting the ability of Iranian manufacturers and farmers to compete) in exchange for loans to pay off the shah's debts. At the same time, the shah gave a British citizen the rights to almost all of Iran's oil fields. The money received for these "sweetheart deals" did little to lower Iran's debt, especially since the shah and his Qajar regime continued to spend lavishly and live far beyond their means.

THE CONSTITUTIONAL REVOLUTION

In the golden era of the Persian Empire, when a ruler was no longer deemed just but was instead found to be working for evil and against the people's best interests, the people felt themselves justified in overthrowing him and replacing him with a true king of kings, a shah who would rule with God and faithfully follow his dictates. At the dawn of the twentieth century, many Iranians felt a similar prompting.

As with the tobacco revolt, merchants, peasants, clerics, and members of the middle class banded together and demanded change. Led by two ayatollahs, the movement grew into a full-scale revolution. The people demanded a halt to the Qajars' disastrous trade policies, a new commitment to sound financial management and spending restraint, and an end to foreign influence and economic meddling. Most important, they demanded a reduction in the power of the monarchy through the drafting of a constitution and the creation of a parliament in which all Iranians could be represented by popularly elected officials.

The revolution was relatively bloodless and, ultimately, successful. In 1906, the shah agreed to the creation of a parliament, known as the Majlis, and he granted the right to vote to all Iranian males who owned property and were over the age of 30. While Iran was still mired in debt, desperately poor, technologically unsophisticated, and manipulated by the leading world powers, its people had struck a major blow for nationalism, sovereignty, and self-rule.

Even more important, the Iranian people had given notice that they would not tolerate inept, corrupt, or tyrannical leadership. They, along with their religious leaders, would have no qualms in deposing leaders deemed to be working against their best interests. This was a dire warning

One of Iran's greatest assets is its abundance of oil. In order to support their lavish lifestyles, Iranian shahs offered British citizens the rights to almost all of Iran's oil fields in exchange for monetary gain. In this 1910 photograph, oil flows from a well at Mastid Sulaiman in Iran.

and a hard lesson that the final shah of Iran, who would rule in the latter half of the twentieth century, would have been wise to heed.

WORLD WAR I AND ITS AFTERMATH

Despite the Iranian people's determination to gain greater control over their nation and its resources, Iran was once again standing on the brink of chaos and exploitation, a victim of global conflict and maneuvering. Soon after the creation of the Majlis, whatever progress the new representative body could achieve towards Iranian sovereignty was negated by the outbreak of World War I in 1914.

Britain's navy had become heavily dependent upon oil as its main fuel source. As a result, the British government acquired a controlling share in the Anglo-Persian Oil Company (APOC), the monopoly that controlled Iranian oil fields. In order to head off Russian competition for this oil-rich Iranian territory, Britain granted Russia control of Istanbul and the Turkish Strait. Iran was to remain technically "neutral" throughout the war, but controlled by Britain.

Yet as the war drew to a close, the country was subject to the intrusive presence of British, Russian, Turkish, and tribal military forces. Agricultural lands were trampled, crops were ruined, irrigation systems were destroyed, and peasants were displaced from their farms. Mass famine resulted, and Iran was plunged into civil unrest. The British, sensing the opportunities that chaos and a power vacuum created, tried to force the Iranian government to accept a treaty that would grant Britain control over Iran's military, its infrastructure, its resources, and its trade. The ruling Qajars, still mired in crushing debt, were willing to sign the treaty, but the Majlis resisted, refusing to agree to it. The British ignored the Majlis' jurisdiction and imposed their control over the beleaguered nation.

IRANIAN DESIRE FOR A RIGHTEOUS LEADER

Once the British sensed that the situation in Iran was far too desperate and chaotic to control, however, they pulled out, leaving a power vacuum to be filled by some charismatic, ambitious Iranian with the necessary nerve, daring, and vision.

In a thousand-years-long cyclical history of repeated falls from glory and resulting trials and tribulations, this postwar period represented one of Iran's lowest, most humiliating ebbs. This mortifying captivity to foreign control and exploitation remains a vivid collective memory for the people of Iran to this day, and most of them vow never to allow their nation to be meddled with and grossly manipulated again.

Regaining control of Iran would require qualities typically associated with the old-time Persian upstarts who emerged from the mountains to found the legendary dynasties of the Persian Empire, men like Cyrus and Darius, and the leaders of the Medes, Achaemenians, Parthians, and Sassanians.

REZA SHAH PAHLAVI

Reza Shah Pahlavi wasn't a leader of the caliber of Cyrus or Darius, but he made a great first impression. Reza Khan, as he was first known, was a tall, fierce-looking commander of the highest status military unit in the Iranian army, the Cossack Brigade, which was once staffed and trained by Russian military officers.

Along with a journalist named Sayyid Zia-al-Din Tabatabai, Reza Khan orchestrated the overthrow of the Qajar regime, after first leading them to believe he was actually protecting them from a growing revolutionary plot. The Qajar shah continued to rule as a figurehead, while Reza Khan was appointed commander of the Iranian army and, later, minister of war and prime minister. Eventually, the Majlis removed the Qajar regime from power, and Reza Khan became shah of Iran, at which point he changed his name to Reza Shah Pahlavi.

Reza Shah, like the great mass of ordinary Iranians, keenly felt the humiliating sting of Iran's recent history of foreign domination and exploitation. He rose to power determined to restore Iran's sovereignty—its control over its own affairs and resources. He was also committed to the idea of modernization. The long years of debt, famine, war, and resource mismanagement under the Qajars had left Iran impoverished and backward. Once the most civilized and advanced empire in the world, it was now a place of drought, ruined fields, crumbling infrastructure, and a technology deficit. It had fallen far behind the Western powers that had raided it for its oil and strategic territories.

Reza Shah engaged in a tricky balancing act. He needed to preserve peace with the world's powers while insisting on his nation's independence. He badly needed the world powers' technological and economic expertise and investment dollars, but he also needed to somehow maintain control of the Iranian economy and natural resources. As a result, he struck delicate, uneasy treaties and agreements with Russia, Britain, and the United States that offered them some economic benefits and limited political influence, but did not require him to sell out his nation's best interests. Having gained more control of Iranian oil fields and negotiated a more fair price for this oil, Reza Shah could use the higher oil revenues to both strengthen his army—the foundation of his power and the best guarantee of its continuing hold—and pursue his modernization program.

REFORM, MODERNIZATION, AND ALIENATION

Reza Shah was the first leader to insist that the nation be referred to as Iran, not Persia, which he felt was an inaccurate term since most Iranians were not ethnic Persians. At the time that he seized control of the country there were only 150 miles of railroad track and 800 miles of roadway. During his reign, he oversaw the building of 14,000 miles of road, 6,000 miles of

Reza Shah Pahlavi poses with three of his children in this 1925 photograph. Reza Shah Pahlavi overthrew the Qajar regime and became a strong leader of Iran. He was responsible for modernizing Iran; strengthening its army; and improving the nation's infrastructure, communication, health care, and education systems. Reza Shah ruled until 1941, when he was forced into exile.

telephone lines, many power plants, the Trans-Iranian Railroad, airline service, and electrical service in all the nation's major cities. He reformed and modernized Iran's banking and health care systems and its civil service, insisted on more favorable trade policies with foreign powers, expanded and improved the education system, and granted women the right to attend university, enter the workforce, and dress in Western styles.

Reza Shah seemed to be getting Iran back on track. He was a strong leader, exerting centralized control over a traditionally fractious nation of many distinct ethnic and tribal groups, and leading his people into the modern world. Yet in doing all of this, Reza Shah had also alienated several important groups.

Though a reformer and a modernizer, Reza Shah was also a ruthless dictator, and a corrupt, bribe-extorting one at that. He profoundly distrusted the workings of democracy. As such, he fixed elections, censored the press, established a secret police force, tortured and killed opponents, and curbed the power, autonomy, and freedom of the Majlis. This angered all the legislators and ordinary Iranians who had fought so hard in the Constitutional Revolution of 1906. Single-mindedly bent on modernization, the shah tended to neglect Iranian agriculture, which was still the most vital part of the national economy.

Finally, the shah saw no place for religion in his vision for a modern, technologically advanced, Westernized Iran. He nullified religious laws and instituted a new civil (nonreligious) law system. He curbed the influence of clerics by seizing control of theological schools. He imposed Western styles of dress. He instituted civil marriages and divorce. This did not sit well with the large number of pious (religious and practicing) Muslims in Iran.

As the entire world became mired in the devastating economic depression of the 1930s and advanced towards a second catastrophic global war, Iran's economy also suffered, and the world's great powers again began eyeing the nation for its oil resources and strategic value. These strains, coupled with the widespread and growing discontent over Reza Shah's harsh, repressive, and uncompromising rule, would result in his downfall.

WORLD WAR II AND REZA SHAH PAHLAVI'S DOWNFALL

In the run-up to World War II, Reza Shah had fallen under the spell of Nazi Germany. He was dazzled by the Nazi regime's industrial power, its military prowess, and its ruthless efficiency and mechanization. Always seeking to secure his own power and autonomy by playing the world powers off of each other, Reza Shah befriended Germany and invited hundreds of businesspeople and political, military, and economic advisers into Iran.

Iran is a valuable and oil-rich link to both the Persian Gulf and the Caspian Sea. It is also an extremely strategic transit route to and from Asia, the Caucuses, the Middle East, and Africa. As such, Russia and Britain, now allied against Germany, could not tolerate this burgeoning friendship between Reza Shah and the leader of Nazi Germany, Adolf Hitler. Russia and Britain demanded that the shah expel all German nationals living in Iran and cede control of the Trans-Iranian Railroad and all Iranian ports to them. Reza Shah refused, making one last doomed stand for his own sovereignty, if not that of his nation's. He was forced into exile on August 25, 1941. His son, Mohammad Reza, only 21 at the time, was named shah in his father's place.

Though not expected to ever be anything other than a puppet of Russia and Britain, Mohammad Reza Shah Pahlavi, as he was now known, would surprise everyone, Iranians included, by seeking to transform himself into a modern-day Persian king of kings, even more ruthlessly determined than his father to create a secular, modern, independent, and autonomous Iran. He would make many of the same enemies as his father, for many of the same reasons—antidemocratic repression, cruelty, corruption, obsessive commitment to modernization despite widespread reluctance, and antireligious secularization of society. He would particularly enrage Iran's Muslim clerics and their legions of passionate followers.

One of these clerics—a humble religious scholar who would go on to become one of the shah's greatest enemies and Iran's supreme leader—was born just two years before Mohammad Reza Shah Pahlavi's reign began. His name was Sayyed Ali Khamenei, and the story of his unlikely rise from poverty, imprisonment, and exile to one of the most important seats of Iranian power begins here.

CHAPTER

4

Ali Khamenei's Youth and Early Education

SAYYED ALI KHAMENEI WAS BORN IN 1939. REPORTS DIFFER ON THE EXACT date of his birth, with some accounts saying July 17 while others claim April 18. He was born in the holy city of Mashhad in Khorasan province, in northeastern Iran. Its name means "place of martyrdom," and it is sometimes described as Iran's holiest city. It was the site of the martyrdom of Imam Reza, the eighth imam of Shiite Islam. He was believed to have been poisoned by a Sunni caliph named Al Ma'mun. The village was small at the time of Imam Reza's death, but a shrine built in his honor soon attracted so many visitors and pilgrims that a city grew up around it. Today, Mashhad is the second largest city in Iran after the capital, Tehran, and is one of the most important pilgrimage destinations for Shiite Muslims, 20 million of whom visit it every year.

"I REMEMBER THAT SOMETIMES AT NIGHT, WE DIDN'T HAVE ANYTHING IN THE HOUSE FOR DINNER."

—Ali Khamenei

FAMILY LIFE

Not only was Khamenei born into Iran's holiest city, he was also born into one of its most pious families. He claims descent from the Prophet Muhammad himself. Both of his grandfathers were renowned clerics, as was his uncle. He was the second son of devout parents. Both his parents were Azeri (or Azerbaijanis), an ethnic group that is generally Muslim and is a mixture of Turkic, Caucasian (from the Caucuses), and Iranian bloodlines and traditions. His father, Sayyed Javad Khamenei, was a humble but well-respected religious scholar who was honored with the responsibility of leading morning, midday, and evening prayers at two of Mashhad's mosques.

Sayyed Javad Khamenei lived a simple life characterized by self-denial and a rejection of worldly goods and luxuries. He kept a bare-bones household and taught all of his children how to live a simple and good life, believing that this freedom from worldly distractions and temptations placed one closer to God and his commandments and in more direct communication with him. On Ali Khamenei's official Web site, he describes his father and his upbringing:

> My father was a well-known religious scholar who was very pious and a bit of a recluse. We had a difficult life. I remember that sometimes at night, we didn't have anything in the house for dinner. Nevertheless, my mother would try to scrape something up, and that dinner would be bread and raisins. . . . My father's house—the one that I was born in and lived in until the age of about four or five—was about a sixty to seventy square meter home located in the poor

Above, evening prayers are held at the Shrine of Imam Reza in Mashhad, the second largest city in Iran and one of the holiest destinations for Shiite Muslims. Every year millions of Shiite Muslims make a pilgrimage to Mashhad, which happens to be Ali Khamenei's birthplace.

area of Mashhad. The house only had one room and a gloomy basement.

The family could afford only barley bread, rather than wheat bread, and it was often bought with the money Ali Khamenei's grandmother gave him and his siblings as a gift. The children's clothes were sewn together from the scraps of their father's worn-out garments. Whenever visitors came to see Sayyed Javad Khamenei, seeking spiritual guidance, the Khamenei children had to retreat to the basement.

Eventually, some friends of his father pooled their resources and bought the Khamenei family a small plot of land adjoining their home, allowing them to put an addition on the house and expand it to three rooms. It is generally believed that Ali Khamenei and his wife and six children lead a similarly simple, pared-down life, even though he has risen to the high rank and status of supreme leader of Iran.

A RELIGIOUS EDUCATION

Given Sayyed Javad Khamenei's emphasis on religion and spirituality, it is no surprise that he enrolled his sons in traditional Islamic religious schools at the earliest possible opportunity, this despite the fact that Iran under Reza Shah Pahlavi and his son Mohammad Reza Shah Pahlavi was becoming more and more secular and Westernized. When Ali Khamenei was four, he and his older brother, Sayyed Muhammad, began attending a *maktab*, a Muslim elementary school. Here, students generally learn reading, writing, and grammar, and study and recite the Koran. These kinds of schools were established by devout Muslims as alternatives to the secular state schools, and they did not enjoy the government's recognition, sanction, or financial support. The Khamenei brothers soon graduated to an Islamic school that was recently opened in Mashhad. Called the Dar al-Ta'leem Diyanat, it offered further elementary education and more high-caliber religious instruction.

RELIGIOUS AND REVOLUTIONARY INSPIRATIONS

Following high school, Khamenei entered the Sulayman Khan Madrassa, a theological seminary in Mashhad. While many of his peers were entering trades or taking professional classes, he had set himself on a religious course. He was studying to become a Muslim cleric. What motivated this decision, according to Khamenei's own words, were his parents' wishes. He claims that the "factor which inspired me to choose the enlightened path of a religious scholar was my father. My mother also encouraged me, as she was very fond of the idea." As quoted by the Islamic Centre of London's biography of Ali Khamenei, he stated that,

> To my father goes the credit of choosing for me the perfect path of knowledge and the *ulema* [Islamic clerical studies]. He instilled in me the eagerness to embark on such a journey. . . . He spared no efforts in making sure that we got our share of his care. He coached my elder brother and I, and afterwards, our younger brother. We are indebted to him for our upbringing and study, especially myself, for had it not been for him, I would not have reached thus far in the fields of acquiring knowledge in *fiqh* [jurisprudence, which is the study of law, the philosophy of law, and the body of court decisions and precedents] and *usul* [principles of jurisprudence].

At the madrassa, Khamenei continued his studies of Arabic grammar and began primary seminary studies. He was instructed and guided in these studies by his father and other prominent and leading religious scholars of Mashhad. During a five-and-a-half year course of intermediate study (a far more accelerated progress than that of most of his fellow seminarians), Khamenei studied logic, philosophy, and Islamic jurisprudence.

It was during his years in the Sulayman Khan Madrassa that Khamenei first felt a powerful call to spread the teachings and influence of Islam. It was not merely a religious impulse, but also a political and revolutionary one. In 1952, a revolutionary cleric named Sayyed Mujtaba Nawwab Safawi visited the madrassa and delivered an angry and spirited sermon denouncing the secular dictatorship of Mohammad

Reza Shah Pahlavi and the ongoing British influence over and involvement in Iranian affairs. He described the nation's rulers as a pack of liars, and the shah and his cohorts as not "true Muslims." He insisted on the importance of reviving Islam in Iranian public and private life and instituting a "Divine Rule," a fundamentalist Islamic government.

Khamenei described this sermon as "music to my ears." On his official Web site, he is quoted as saying, "It was at that very moment, because of Nawwab Safawi, that the consciousness of Islamic Revolutionary activism sparked inside me. I have no doubt that it was Nawwab Safawi who first kindled the fire in my heart." Nawwab Safawi would later be executed by the shah's agents, yet this did nothing to dampen the revolutionary fire burning in Khamenei's breast. It only seemed to stiffen his resolve to do battle with the shah and wage a holy war designed to install an Islamist government in Iran. The threat of violence and death that lay down this path left him undaunted.

5

Khomeini's Revolutionary Movement

AT THE STARTLINGLY YOUNG AGE OF 18, ALI KHAMENEI FINISHED HIS intermediate studies and began the highest level of study of Islamic jurisprudence under the Grand Ayatollah Milani, one of the most high-ranking and influential clerics of the time in Iran. That same year, Khamenei decided to visit some of the most important holy sites in neighboring Iraq. As a result, he traveled to the city of Najaf, 100 miles south of Iraq's capital, Baghdad.

Najaf is considered a holy city because it contains the tomb of Ali ibn Abi Talib, whom Shiite Muslims believe to be a righteous caliph and the first imam. Najaf also contains the Imam Ali mosque—a stunning gilded and domed building dedicated to Ali ibn Abi Talib—and the largest cemetery in the Muslim world. It is believed to be the third most popular Muslim pilgrimage site behind Mecca and Medina in Saudi Arabia. As such, Najaf has attracted many Islamic scholars and devout Muslims and has developed into the main center of Shiite theological studies.

While in Najaf, Khamenei visited the city's seminary and fell under the sway of some of its leading teachers and ayatollahs. He describes feeling an overpowering urge to stay and continue his studies there. He was allowed to remain only about a year, however, before his father expressed his desire that Khamenei return to Iran for his clerical education. Sayyed Javad Khamenei had decided that his son should instead study in the Iranian holy city of Qom, about 100 miles southwest of Tehran.

Like both Mashhad and Najaf, Qom is a major pilgrimage site and a place held sacred by Shiite Muslims. It contains the shrine of Fatema Mae'sume, the sister of Imam Ali ibn Musa Rida, the eighth imam of Shi'ah Islam. Qom would also become the main base of operations for Khomeini's Islamist revolutionary movement in opposition to the shah's rule in the 1960s and 1970s, a revolutionary movement that would include Khamenei at its center.

IRAN UNDER THE SHAH

In fact, it was in the seminary at Qom that Khamenei first met and received the patronage of Ayatollah Khomeini. From 1958 to 1964, Khamenei studied under Khomeini, as well as other leading ayatollahs and teachers. In 1962, he officially joined Khomeini's revolutionary movement.

Khomeini and his Islamist followers were dedicated to the overthrow of Mohammad Reza Shah Pahlavi, who was widely despised for the brutality of his dictatorship, his aggressively antireligious secularism, his modernization program that many Muslims believe trampled upon holy traditions and Islamic principles, his creation of a ruling class of wealthy and

Iranian army tanks stand in front of the central police headquarters after the attempted coup d'etat against Iranian prime minister Mohammad Mosaddegh. The U.S. Central Intelligence Agency supported the coup because the prime minister was opposed to Western control of Iranian oil fields. The long history of Iranian resentment and distrust of the United States dates back to the coup of 1953.

influential businesspeople, and his courting of Western powers, particularly Britain and the United States.

The shah had abolished multiparty rule and forced all Iranians to join his party, the *Rastakhiz* ("Resurrection"). With the help of the U.S. Central Intelligence Agency (CIA), he created a brutal secret police and intelligence agency, the SAVAK, whose agents secretly imprisoned, tortured, and even executed and assassinated political opponents. The CIA also most likely supported and assisted in the 1953 "coup" against the independent-minded prime minister, Mohammad Mosaddegh, a powerful opponent of the shah and a vocal critic of Western control of Iranian oil fields and appropriation of oil profits. This instance of American meddling in support of the shah is one of the primary sources of Iranian rage and hatred for America.

Most important, the shah angered conservative, pious Muslims by granting the right to vote to women, strongly encouraging Western styles of dress, seizing control over seminaries and clerical examinations, and maintaining friendly relations with Israel.

Most Islamic clerics and many of the Iranian people, weary of both Iran's recent past of experiencing foreign meddling and exploitation, and its far longer history of invasion and conquest, had reached the end of their patience with leaders who did not represent the nation's best interests and those of its people. Hearkening back to the ancient Zoroastrian traditions, many Iranians concluded that Mohammad Reza Shah Pahlavi was a "bad king" who did not speak for God, did not wage war against evil, and did not fight for good on behalf of his subjects. He, in fact, was seen as an agent of evil, serving the "Great Satan"—the source of all evil in the world, the United States. Therefore, he had to be deposed and replaced by a righteous and just ruler. That man was deemed by an increasingly large segment of the Iranian population to be Ayatollah Khomeini.

ALI KHAMENEI JOINS THE REVOLUTIONARY MOVEMENT

Ayatollah Khomeini urged his followers in the Qom seminary to do everything they could to spread his message of radical Islamist revolution to other seminaries in Iran and throughout the entire nation to ordinary Iranians. Because Khamenei had such strong links to the seminary in his hometown, Ayatollah Khomeini sent him to Mashhad to convey his message of revolution to his former teacher, Ayatollah Milani, and all the clerics, teachers, and students at Sulayman Khan Madrassa and throughout the province of Khorasan. This was Khamenei's first official act in support of the revolutionary movement, and the message he carried was meant to expose the alleged evils of the shah's regime and suggest ways in which Islamist resistance could grow and spread, ultimately resulting in the toppling of the shah.

During his mission to Khorasan province, Khamenei visited the city of Birjand, considered to be one of the shah's strongholds and the home of his prime minister, Asadullah Alam. In this city so closely allied with the shah's regime, Khamenei dared to deliver a series of inflammatory sermons denouncing the shah, his policies and phony "reforms," and the social and spiritual ills of Iran under the rule of Mohammad Reza Shah Pahlavi.

ARRESTS AND DEFIANCE

After delivering several of these sermons, agents of the shah moved in and arrested Khamenei. He was held overnight and transferred to Mashhad, where he was imprisoned for 10 days and subjected to hard labor. Yet Khamenei remained unintimidated and defiant: "Jail was not bad. It was a new experience. It was a different world, that of the SAVAK and its interrogation procedures and wounding insults—in short, the pain of struggle" (as quoted by the English Islamic Centre). As Khamenei himself realized, he was now on the shah's radar and would be under constant watch by SAVAK agents. His life as a humble, anonymous, soft-spoken seminary student was over. Khamenei was now an Islamist revolutionary.

Demonstrating his undiminished and unbroken revolutionary spirit, the first thing Khamenei did upon being released from prison was to meet with fellow followers of Ayatollah Khomeini to discuss strategy and plan their next move. They decided to split up and spread out throughout Iran, visiting as many cities, towns, and villages as possible and spreading Khomeini's message of resistance to the shah's supposedly anti-Islam, pro-American regime. Khamenei was sent to Kerman, almost 700 miles south of Tehran. There he met with clerics, seminary students, and so-called *mujahideen*, or holy warriors—men willing to fight and die for the radical Islamist cause. He also delivered several more fiery sermons of the type he delivered in Birjand.

From Kerman, Khamenei traveled to Zahedan in southeastern Iran, near the border with Pakistan. In the city's main mosque, he delivered more antigovernment tirades over several days. These were provocative enough to again prompt SAVAK agents to move in and arrest him. He was flown to Tehran and imprisoned for two months in Qizil Qala'a prison, a place greatly feared by enemies of the shah's regime. Khamenei was placed in solitary confinement, verbally abused, tortured, and threatened with execution.

Upon his release, Khamenei returned to Qom, where Ayatollah Khomeini was under house arrest. Reportedly, the first thing Khamenei did upon arriving in the city after his two months in prison was to visit Khomeini. He had said that, "Seeing the Imam, I felt all tiredness and pain vanish from my body. I cried out from the joy of seeing him" (as quoted by the English Islamic Centre). Khomeini, often viewed as a stern, sour man, even joked with his pupil as they discussed the next step in their shared march toward revolution.

A SON'S DUTY

Soon after returning to the seminary and resuming his studies and his revolutionary indoctrination, however, Khamenei received troubling news from home. His father had lost sight in one eye due to cataracts (clouding of the lens of the eye and surrounding membrane) and could no longer read. Khamenei, who felt he owed so much to his father and his loving care and tutelage, decided it was his duty to return to Mashhad and care for the aging cleric. His teachers and fellow seminarians were said to be dismayed by this decision, believing one of the seminary's brightest, most promising pupils—and one of its most articulate, fiery messengers of revolution—was abandoning his studies and political activities.

Yet Khamenei, though determined to go home and help his family, was in no way interested in neglecting either his ongoing religious education and training or his revolutionary activities. Once back in Mashhad, he continued to study under his old master, Ayatollah Milani, and other of the city's leading teachers. He also began to teach Islamic jurisprudence and theology to younger students. In 1964, Khomeini himself would also leave Qom after being arrested by SAVAK agents and sent into exile. Khomeini would spend the next 14 years outside of Iran, mostly in Najaf, Iraq.

It was in this capacity as teacher that Khamenei was able to resume his revolutionary activities and spread Ayatollah Khomeini's message of Islamic radicalism and anti-shah agitation. Khamenei's lectures—delivered in Mashhad and Tehran—on the Koran, the prophetic traditions, Islamic ideology, and jurisprudence were infused with Khomeini's revolutionary principles. The overriding message was that the shah's corrupt, godless regime must be overthrown.

BUILDING ALLIANCES, DISGUISING TRUE INTENTIONS

Ayatollah Khomeini was careful to attract as many anti-shah followers as possible—including moderate Muslims, secular

Iranian students and supporters in this 1978 photograph surround Ayatollah Khomeini, leader of the revolutionary movement against the shah of Iran. One of Khomeini's supporters was Ali Khamenei, who went on missions to denounce the shah of Iran. Due to his sermons condemning the shah, Khamenei was arrested repeatedly by the shah's secret police.

Iranians, and communist and socialist militants (communists generally do not believe in God and are often hostile to religion)—so he downplayed his desire to establish an Islamist leadership and cleric-dominated government structure once the shah was toppled. He often spoke favorably of principles like "democracy" and "freedom." Khomeini needed to create a critical mass of opposition, but once his goal of removing the shah was achieved, he intended to split from those members of the revolution who did not share his vision of an Islamist Iran.

Yet in written messages and sermons delivered to their pious Muslim followers in mosques and seminaries around the country, Khomeini and Ali Khamenei argued that the coming revolution was God's will, and the new government and its people would be free to act in exact accordance with God's will, not that of the corrupt shah or his evil American sponsors. It was clear to Khomeini's fundamentalist followers that, following the removal of the shah, he intended to establish *sharia* law in Iran—a system of law based on Islamic jurisprudence and interpretations of the Koran's moral and spiritual precepts.

GOING UNDERGROUND

In the mid-1960s, Ayatollah Khomeini decided to organize his followers into secret cells. These small groups of several revolutionary clerics and students would be scattered throughout the nation and spread Khomeini's message. In 1966, however, following the arrest of a radical cleric, Ayatollah Azeri Qumi, the existence, organization, and membership of these cells were discovered by SAVAK agents searching Qumi's house. During interrogation, Qumi was tortured and may have given up some names of fellow revolutionaries, who were then arrested.

Many of the remaining cell members, including Khamenei, went into hiding. For one year, he hid out with fellow cleric Ayatollah Ali Rafsanjani, who would later share power with Khamenei in post-revolutionary Iran. In a meeting he held with Rafsanjani and two other revolutionary clerics, it was decided that all cell members must remain in hiding and never appear in public. Khamenei realized he could not return to Mashhad, his family, or his studies for the foreseeable future.

Towards the end of 1966, some of the cell members who had been arrested were released from prison. This emboldened the revolutionaries who had gone into hiding, including

Khamenei, who promptly returned to Mashhad. Though the stated purpose of his visit was a pilgrimage to the city's holy shrine honoring Imam Reza, Khamenei quickly began delivering anti-shah sermons and lectures to students and ordinary Iranians. In 1967, he was again arrested by the SAVAK and briefly imprisoned. He claims to have been again tortured in jail but refused to reveal any information about the revolutionary activities of Ayatollah Khomeini's movement or its membership. He was soon released and returned to Mashhad, where he resumed teaching theology and Koran studies to seminary students, a radical Islamist message always folded within his lessons.

FINDING HIS VOICE

These sermons and lectures struck a chord with fellow clerics, students, and average Iranians, and soon people were traveling from all over Iran to hear Khamenei speak. Naturally, this alerted and alarmed the SAVAK, who had him under almost constant surveillance. SAVAK agents frequently interrupted and canceled his classes, which Khamenei began holding in many locations to keep his pursuers off balance. The more he was pursued and harassed, the more he became something of a people's hero, an object of sympathy and admiration.

Khamenei was invited to give lectures to many different Islamic societies, seminaries, and other centers of learning throughout the nation, during which he always delivered a withering critique of the shah's regime, his pro-American policies and attitudes, and his contempt for Islam. During this period, Khamenei also accepted several offers to become the imam of various mosques in Mashhad, where his responsibilities were teaching, preaching, and the leading of prayers. This gave him yet another platform for delivering Khomeini's revolutionary message. In addition to his growing lecture circuit, Khamenei was also now writing and publishing books, which spread the word of his and Ayatollah Khomeini's brand of Islamic radicalism even farther, reaching many more people.

BUILDING REVOLUTIONARY PRESSURE AND FURTHER IMPRISONMENT

All of this activity brought him to the attention of several armed revolutionary groups, who contacted him and explored areas of cooperation. When one of these groups detonated a bomb during official government celebrations of the 2,500th anniversary of Iranian monarchy in 1971, Ali Khamenei was one of the suspects rounded up and imprisoned. Once again he claims to have suffered abuse and torture during the detention, and, once again, upon his release, he remained unbowed and simply picked up where he left off, denouncing the shah and preaching revolution.

For the next few years, SAVAK agents regularly monitored, harassed, detained, and interrogated Khamenei, interrupting his classes and shutting down the mosques in which he preached and led prayers. Yet, to counteract these disruptions, his lectures were handwritten or printed and distributed throughout Iran. Similarly, Khamenei's students fanned out throughout the nation to share the content of his lectures and sermons to an Iranian public increasingly disenchanted with the shah's rule.

In 1975, Khamenei was arrested again after SAVAK agents stormed into his home. This would prove to be both his most serious brush with the shah's security forces and his final imprisonment. Khomeini, Khamenei, and their fellow revolutionary clerics had been so successful in stirring up the Iranian populace and tapping into widespread discontent with the shah's regime that matters were coming to a head. Unrest and open talk of revolution were rising. The shah believed a crackdown was necessary. As quoted in the biography on Khamenei's official web site, he says,

[T]he situation was ripening for an armed revolution in Iran. The sensitivity and severity of the former regime against me had increased. Because of the circumstances, they were no longer able to ignore people such as myself. . . . The harsh attitude of SAVAK indicated that the System was very afraid of an armed revolution being accompanied with a sound Islamic ideology. They could no longer believe that my intellectual activism and propagation in Mashhad and Tehran had nothing to do with the developing situation.

The time for student "awakening" and secret cells and intermittent government harassment was over. The revolutionary movement was out in the open and increasingly vocal, and the government's reaction was equally blunt and undisguised.

What followed for Khamenei was a year of extremely harsh imprisonment. Sometimes he was in solitary confinement. Sometimes he was placed in a cell with several other prisoners and allegedly tortured. Prisoners were said to have been beaten to the point of unconsciousness, then revived, only to be beaten again. Khamenei's beard was shaved, his turban was removed, and he was routinely slapped on the cheek, all of which are considered to be grave humiliations by pious Muslims.

When Jimmy Carter was elected to the U.S. presidency in 1976, he took office the following year determined to alter America's relationship with Iran. A liberal Democrat who was firmly committed to human rights, Carter was very uneasy with the repressive and brutal nature of Mohammad Reza Shah Pahlavi's regime. Though reliant on access to Iran's oil and therefore forced to maintain the longstanding "friendship" between the U.S. and the shah, Carter tried to use his moral authority to exert pressure on the Iranian government to improve its human rights record. As a result, some political prisoners, even those actively agitating against the shah's rule, were released from prison. One of these men was Ali Khamenei.

CHAPTER

6

The Iranian Revolution

ALI KHAMENEI RETURNED ONCE AGAIN TO MASHHAD AND, UNREPENTANT, continued his revolutionary activities. He had plenty of time to focus on these efforts since he was now banned from teaching and preaching. In 1977, from his exile in Najaf, Iraq, Ayatollah Khomeini established ties with mujahideen groups in Iran— armed militant Islamic militias who shared the radical clerics' anti-shah passion.

Khomeini decided to again organize secret revolutionary cells, each one composed of mujahideen members and led by radical clerics. Ali Khamenei was one of five clerics who met to discuss and orchestrate the formation of these cells. This new militant organization became known as the Mujahideen Ulema League (an *ulema* is a cleric). The league was able to organize many mass marches and protests in Iran in 1977 and 1978, further raising the heat on the shah's regime and building the revolutionary pressure.

EXILE

Ali Khamenei's renewed radical activities did not go unnoticed by the SAVAK. Once again, in 1977, he was taken into custody. Instead of being imprisoned again, however, he, like his mentor and leader Ayatollah Khomeini, was forced into exile. Khamenei was sent to Iranshahr, a city in southeastern Iran. Even in this remote frontier city, however, he was able to continue working towards the shah's overthrow. He courted local mujahideen and brought together rival Shiite and Sunni groups to join the revolutionary struggle. Following a devastating series of rains and floods, he organized local seminary students into a relief committee. Having won the hearts and minds of flood victims, Khamenei used the committee to spread Ayatollah Khomeini's anti-shah message to a newly receptive and grateful audience. Though exiled, Khamenei forced SAVAK agents to keep a close eye on him.

The seeds of revolution so painstakingly planted by Ayatollah Khomeini, Ali Khamenei, and other radical clerics began to burgeon in 1978. Protests and mass rallies consumed Tehran and other Iranian cities, and the shah's regime began to lose its tight grip on the nation. Amid the growing chaos and the SAVAK's divided attention, Khamenei ended his exile without official permission. He sneaked back to Mashhad and became one of six radical clerics handpicked by Khomeini—who was now living in exile in Paris, France—to form and head up the Revolutionary Command Council.

THE REVOLUTIONARY COMMAND COUNCIL

The Revolutionary Command Council would come to include anti-shah political figures who did not share Ayatollah's Khomeini's vision for an Islamist Iran. They believed they had formed a coalition of interest groups intent on toppling the shah and then forming a unity government composed of power-sharing factions. Khomeini's speeches had often mentioned "democracy" and "freedom." Khomeini, however, was

Ayatollah Hussein Ali Montazeri, president of Iran's Revolutionary Command Council, holds a bayonet as he addresses a rally at Tehran University in 1979. Ali Khamenei was a member of the Revolutionary Command Council and was known for his participation in rallies and his passionate speeches. Khamenei was a vital member of the council.

only interested in exploiting these politicians' authority and power base long enough to bring about revolution. Once the shah was deposed, he intended to fill the power vacuum and

SIXTY-THREE U.S. EMBASSY EMPLOYEES WERE HELD IN TEHRAN FOR 444 DAYS WITH KHOMEINI'S BLESSING AND ALI KHAMENEI'S VOCAL SUPPORT.

establish an absolutist religious regime based upon Koranic principles and precepts.

After being appointed to the Revolutionary Command Council, Khamenei left Mashhad for Tehran and helped organize more mass protest marches in Iran's capital city and in his home province of Khorasan, where he was one of the most prominent and passionate speakers.

THE END OF THE SHAH

This building pressure, anger, protest, and outrage finally built to a breaking point, as large numbers of soldiers began to desert and defect from the shah's army. Mohammad Reza Shah Pahlavi, recognizing the near certainty of a coup and fearing for his and his family's lives, fled Iran on January 16, 1979.

Widely despised throughout the Middle East for his friendship with the United States and Israel, and unpopular with much of the rest of the world for his poor human rights record, the shah and his wife bounced from country to country in a globe-trotting exile. He first went to Egypt, then Morocco, the Bahamas, Mexico, and finally the United States. President Carter had been unwilling to offer him asylum because of his murderous reputation, but at this point the shah was suffering from terminal cancer.

For humanitarian reasons, Carter allowed the former shah of Iran to enter the United States for medical treatment, an action that was used as the justification for the Iranian hostage crisis of 1979–1981, in which 63 U.S. embassy employees were held hostage in Tehran for 444 days with Khomeini's

The shah of Iran poses with his family in the Bahamas in this 1979 photograph. Due to political unrest and Khomeini's revolutionary movement, the shah and his family fled Iran and went on a worldwide exile. Mohammad Reza Pahlavi, shah of Iran, died on July 27, 1980, from non-Hodgkin's lymphoma.

blessing and Ali Khamenei's vocal support. The radical pro-Khomeini university students who had taken the Americans hostage demanded the shah's return to Iran so he could be put on trial and executed for crimes against the nation. Though the shah left the United States in December 1979, the hostage crisis dragged on until early 1981, when the students released the Americans mere minutes after Ronald Reagan replaced Jimmy Carter as U.S. president. After leaving the United States, the shah briefly stayed in Panama, then returned to Egypt, where he died on July 27, 1980.

THE AYATOLLAH'S TRIUMPHANT RETURN AND RUTHLESS POWER GRAB

While the last shah of Iran was wandering the world— disgraced, deathly ill, and exiled—Ayatollah Khomeini ended his exile in Paris and received a hero's welcome in Iran upon his return on February 1, 1979. In less than two weeks, he replaced the interim pro-democracy prime minister with someone of his own choosing, and he convinced many members of the Iranian armed forces to join his cause. The army, sensing the sea change underway, remained officially neutral and allowed Khomeini to seize the reins of power. By the end of March, a referendum (popular polling of citizens) resulted in the official dismantling of the centuries-old Iranian monarchy, creating a republic in its place (an elected government led by a president or prime minister, instead of a royal figure).

In the early post-revolution days, Ayatollah Khomeini promised Iranians that he would establish a democracy—a popularly elected government free of clerical rule or any form of tyranny and repression. Yet within a few months of his triumphant return to Iran, Khomeini set about purging the provisional government of his former liberal and secu-lar revolutionary allies and shutting down many newspaper offices. He declared his intention to set up a theocracy— a government ruled by religious leaders whose authority is said to come directly from God and whose policies are thought to be divinely inspired and mandated (thereby making political opposition among believers nearly impossible).

Trusting in the persuasive power of his charisma and enormous popularity, he had the audacity to present his imposition of a repressive theocracy as a blessing for the

THE OFFICE OF SUPREME LEADER, WHICH WAS DESIGNED BY AND FOR KHOMEINI HIMSELF, GRANTED HIM NEARLY UNLIMITED POWERS OVER THE GOVERNMENT AND PEOPLE OF IRAN.

people that would avert national and spiritual disaster. Of his pro-democracy political opponents and critics, he said, "They want to make a Western country for you in which you will be free, you will be independent, but in which there is no God. This will lead to our destruction" (as quoted in Ray Takeyh's book *Hidden Iran*).

Khomeini rewrote the republic's interim constitution to create both the new position of *faqih*, or supreme leader (to be filled by an ayatollah), and a Council of Guardians (also stocked with clerics) who had the power to veto any law passed by the Majlis that was deemed to be in violation of Islamic precepts. An Assembly of Experts was also created. This was a popularly elected body of clerics that chose the nation's supreme leader, supervised his words and actions, and dismissed him if necessary (for reasons of health, ideology, or qualifications). Khomeini tampered with the election process and loaded the assembly with his own loyalists. As a result, he was easily chosen as the Iranian republic's first supreme leader (a lifetime appointment, barring dismissal) in November 1979 and was further declared the "Leader of the Revolution."

SUPREME LEADER

The office of supreme leader, which was designed by and for Khomeini himself, granted him nearly unlimited powers over the government and people of Iran. He was given command over the army and Revolutionary Guards. He could dismiss

After spending 14 years in exile, Ayatollah Khomeini returned to Iran on February 1, 1979, after Mohammad Reza Pahlavi, shah of Iran, fled the country. Khomeini led the Iranian Revolution and became the Iranian supreme leader. He transformed Iran from a monarchy to an Islamic republic and remained in power until his death in 1989.

any elected official, veto any law passed by the Majlis, and declare war and peace without the advice and consent of elected representatives of the people. Khomeini could only be removed by the Assembly of Experts, but he had made sure to stock that group with loyalists who would never dare to oppose or betray him.

In effect, the supreme leader also had near total control over the press and mass media, including television, radio, and newspapers. If the organizations that produced news and entertainment did not reflect the republic's revolutionary Islamic ideals, they could be shut down. Khomeini also forged a close relationship with the *bonyads*—large foundations run by the Iranian business elite that control most of the money and economic and commercial activity in Iran. They were answerable only to the supreme leader but otherwise were given free rein to conduct business. In exchange, they threw their considerable power and influence behind Khomeini and his movement, protecting him from any rebelliousness among the political opposition or the people.

ESTABLISHING A THEOCRACY

Having granted himself nearly absolute power, Khomeini quickly set about to impose sharia law and roll back the shah's longstanding policies of secularization and social liberalization. Reversing the shah's insistence upon Western styles of dress, Khomeini instituted mandatory Islamic dress codes, including veils and covered heads for women. Men were not allowed to wear shorts, and women always had to wear socks and loose-fitting pants, dresses, coats, and jackets. A woman's ankles and hair must never be exposed, and the shape and contours of her body had to be carefully hidden. Women could not ride bicycles, and unmarried men and women could not dance or hold hands in public and had to be chaperoned when out on dates. Pop music and American and European films were banned.

All schools and universities adopted an Islamic curriculum. Former members of the shah's regime, along with former allies of Khomeini—including communists, socialists, and pro-democracy students and politicians—were rounded up, imprisoned, and, in thousands of cases, executed. Newspapers that expressed opposition to Khomeini and his anti-democratic policies were shut down, their editors arrested. Members of some religious minorities were denied jobs and entrance to universities and, in some cases, persecuted and imprisoned. Muslim converts to other religions could even be executed. Many of these human rights violations continue to this day under Ali Khamenei's leadership.

Khomeini's theocracy was turning out to be every bit as repressive, antidemocratic, dictatorial, and violent as the shah's regime, despite the Ayatollah's many years of withering moral and religious condemnation of his predecessor. There is no reason to believe that Ali Khamenei had any reservations about the progress of the post-revolutionary Islamic Republic of Iran. If he felt any qualms about Khomeini's tactics or his definition of "justice" and "righteousness," he certainly kept them to himself and continued to play the role of the star pupil and loyal assistant.

7

President Ali Khamenei

IN KHOMEINI'S EYES, THE REVOLUTION WAS NOW COMPLETE. THE SHAH WAS overthrown, he had seized power and purged his enemies and former allies alike, and he had created a theocratic state, ruled by sharia law and dominated by his close allies and committed followers. He had won, and his vision of an Islamist Iran was now a reality. Now he could turn his attention to rewarding those clerics and supporters who had fought alongside him for more than 15 years of harassment, imprisonment, torture, and exile. And in rewarding them with important government appointments, he was also ensuring that he maintained a tight grip on power. One of the first clerics he showed his favor and gratitude to was Ali Khamenei, his longtime star pupil and trusted revolutionary.

Between 1979 and 1990, through Khomeini's appointments and endorsement, Khamenei served in increasingly important and influential positions, including:

- Founding member of the Islamic Republic Party (founded by many of the same revolutionary clerics who had formed the Revolutionary Command Council).
- Secretary general of the Islamic Republic Party.
- Deputy minister of defense.
- Supervisor of the Islamic Revolutionary Guards (the republic's largest military organization; among other things, Khamenei was responsible for the religious and ideological indoctrination of the Iranian military).
- Leader of Tehran's Friday congregational prayers.
- Tehran's representative in the Majlis.
- Khomeini's representative on the Supreme Defense Council (one of his duties was the personal, on-site review of the frontlines during the Iran-Iraq War of 1980–1988).
- Chairman of the Cultural Revolution Council.
- President of the Expediency Council (which mediates and resolves disputes between the Majlis and the Council of Guardians and advises the supreme leader).
- Chairman of the Committee for the Revision of the Constitution.

Yet none of these positions of authority and influence came close to the seats of power that Ali Khamenei would ultimately occupy.

POLITICAL ASSASSINATIONS AND ALI KHAMENEI'S BRUSH WITH DEATH

Having turned on and attacked his former Marxist allies in the wake of the revolution, Ayatollah Khomeini and his theocratic government became the target of armed communist militias and terrorist groups. In the early 1980s, a wave of bombings and assassination attempts—launched mainly by Mujahideen-e-Khalq, a group of Marxist radicals—killed more than 70 of Iran's ruling clerics and politicians.

Along with Ali Khamenei, Hashemi Rafsanjani *(above)* had a more liberal stance on Iran's foreign policy. The two men believed that Iran should forge a relationship with Western countries in order to gain weapons and support for its war against Iraq. At that time, the United States was also secretly sending support to Iraq.

Ali Khamenei himself was seriously wounded by a bomb hidden in a tape recorder during a sermon he was delivering at a mosque south of Tehran in June 1981. He was hospitalized for several months and suffered permanent damage to his arm, vocal chords, and lungs.

In the hospital, Khamenei received a telegram from Ayatollah Khomeini himself. As quoted in the the English Islamic Centre's biography of Ali Khamenei it read, in part:

> Anti-revolutionary forces have attacked you, not for any crime you have committed but because you are a loyal soldier at the front, a teacher in the prayer niche, an eloquent orator in [Friday] and congregational prayers, and a faithful guide in the arena of the revolution.

Ali Khamenei was no doubt cheered and moved by this high praise from his mentor and idol. Far from daunted or shaken by the assassination attempt, Khamenei interpreted his survival as proof of the great responsibilities and glorious destiny that still lay ahead for him: "Right from the assassination attempt on my life, I had a feeling that Allah had chosen me for a great task for which I had been prepared. At the time, I did not know the nature of the task. However, I had no doubt that I should be ready to shoulder a great weight in His way for the sake of the revolution" (as quoted by the English Islamic Centre's biography).

Ali Khamenei was correct in sensing that a new task and solemn duty was about to be thrust upon him. The wave of assassinations unleashed by the Mujahideen-e-Khalq claimed the lives of Iran's prime minister, Mohammad Javad Bahonar, and its president, Mohammad Ali Rajai (who had been president for only two weeks after serving as prime minister). Both men were Khomeini loyalists and committed to the revolution. They had both been involved in the post-revolution effort to purge Iranian universities of European and American influences.

THE PRESIDENCY AND A MOVE TOWARDS MODERATION

With the office of the presidency vacant, Ayatollah Khomeini moved quickly to fill it. He turned to one of his most trusted and loyal assistants—Ali Khamenei—and urged the ruling clerics in the Council of Guardians to approve him as a presidential candidate. Ali Khamenei was elected by a large majority (95 percent) of the Iranian people in early October 1981 and became the third president of the republic. He was the first cleric to hold the office. Khomeini had originally claimed he wished to keep the presidency free of clerical influence, but he must have come to recognize the value of having one of his closest loyalists in this seat of power. Having Ali Khamenei serve as president allowed Ayatollah Khomeini to consolidate his power and gain an even tighter grip on the nation and its government.

For the most part, Khamenei's two terms as president of the republic—he was reelected in 1985—were unremarkable from a political and policy standpoint. He closely toed Khomeini's conservative Islamist line and rarely challenged the ayatollah's viewpoint. He did get into sharp policy disagreements with Iran's socialist-leaning prime minister, Hussein Moussavi (who was selected by the Majlis over Khomeini's hand-picked candidate). Most of these disputes related to Moussavi's desire to enact radical land and business reform that would redistribute wealth from the hands of wealthy merchants and landed elites to working-class and peasant Iranians. Most of these questions were resolved by the conservative Council of Guardians in favor of Ali Khamenei's viewpoint (and by extension, that of Khomeini).

Yet Khamenei did begin to earn a reputation as a pragmatic cleric who represented a slightly more moderate stance than that of Ayatollah Khomeini. In partnership with the speaker of the Majlis, Ali Akbar Hashemi Rafsanjani, Ali Khamenei urged a more liberal foreign policy than that advocated by Khomeini and the hard-line senior clerics. He believed that Iran needed

RAFSANJANI HAMMERED OUT A SECRET DEAL WITH THE ADMINISTRATION OF U.S. PRESIDENT RONALD REAGAN IN 1985 TO OBTAIN DESPERATELY NEEDED WEAPONS FOR ITS WAR WITH IRAQ.

to end its worldwide isolation by improving relations with the nations of the world, especially those countries that could benefit and enrich Iran through trade.

In theory, Khamenei and Rafsanjani argued, Iran should be able to develop relations with any nation—including the "Great Satan," the United States—if the relationship was based on respect and reciprocity. Indeed, Rafsanjani hammered out a secret deal with the administration of U.S. president Ronald Reagan in 1985 to obtain desperately needed weapons for its war with Iraq (despite the fact that the United States was also secretly aiding Iraqi forces). Iran would also no longer try to export its Islamic revolution through calls to violent uprising in Muslim nations, but instead would inspire by example and encourage peaceful transitions to Islamic rule throughout the Middle East. Surprisingly, Ayatollah Khomeini was said to have supported this new foreign policy initiative, despite its moderation.

THE IRAN-IRAQ WAR

Ali Khamenei further demonstrated moderate tendencies when he, again in partnership with Speaker Rafsanjani, supported an end to the eight-year Iran-Iraq War without achieving military victory. This war had begun in 1980 when Iraqi president Saddam Hussein, sensing weakness and chaos in post-revolution Iran and intent upon seizing control of some Iranian territory and oil fields, invaded his neighbor. Hussein and his regime were Sunni Muslims, and this invasion rekindled Iranians' vivid and bitter memories of their

Pictured above is a 1986 *Time* magazine cover exposing the secret relationship between the United States and Iran. Ali Akbar Hashemi Rafsanjani was responsible for creating a deal with the United States, who would supply Iran with weapons for its war with Iraq.

centuries-long history of invasions and conquests, and the intense loathing that sprang from Sunni Arab rule following the Muslim invasion and forced conversion of Persia. Fired by their renewed sense of ancient wrongs and emboldened by a zealous nationalism in the wake of the revolution and establishment of the republic, millions of young Iranians rushed to the front and fought for their god and their country.

As the war ground on, however, and casualties mounted to, by some estimates, as high as a million, more and more Iranians realized that victory remained distant and a solution had to be reached. Over the protests of senior clerics, Ali Khamenei and Speaker Rafsanjani spoke to Khomeini and convinced him to agree to an end to hostilities. On July 20, 1988, as quoted in Kenneth M. Pollack's book *The Persian Puzzle*, Ayatollah Khomeini issued a statement to the nation, saying,

> I had promised to fight to the last drop of my blood and to my last breath. Taking this decision was more deadly than drinking hemlock. I submitted myself to God's will and drank this drink for His satisfaction. To me, it would have been more bearable to accept death and martyrdom. Today's decision is based only on the interest of the Islamic Republic.

Though Khomeini had long vowed to die before giving up the fight with Iraq, he bowed to reality, recognizing that the republic he had fought to establish could crumble if the war were to continue.

THE LIMITS OF POWER

Ali Khamenei's moderating viewpoint could only go so far, however, and as president, he could only do so much. The Guardians and Khomeini had the real power, since the prime minister and the Majlis were subject to their veto, and no one dared cross the larger-than-life, enormously revered supreme

(From left to right) Ali Khameini, an Iranian official, Khomeini's son Ahmad, and Ali Akbar Hashemi Rafsanjani all mourn the death of Ayatollah Khomeini. The death of Iran's first supreme leader left the country in grief. Following Khomeini's passing, Ali Khameini became Iran's second supreme leader.

ruler. The presidency offered Khamenei very little real authority. The position mainly served to create the illusion of a balance of power in the Iranian government and that some kind of system of checks and balances was in place.

The conservative clerics of the Council of Guardians—six of whom are appointed by the supreme leader, the other six appointed by the head of the judiciary who, in turn, is appointed by the supreme leader—had all the leverage, and

WHOEVER FOLLOWED KHOMEINI AS SUPREME LEADER WOULD HAVE ENORMOUS SHOES TO FILL.

the president merely served a largely ceremonial role. It is unlikely, however, that Ali Khamenei would have advocated any policies greatly differing from Khomeini's conservative Islamic program if he had been granted the freedom to do so. He was a true protégé of the ayatollah and had no apparent desire to blaze his own trail.

THE DEATH OF AYATOLLAH KHOMEINI

Yet the time was drawing near when Ali Khamenei—and all of Iran—would have to continue down the road of national destiny without the rigid guidance and iron leadership of Ayatollah Khomeini. Terminally ill from cancer and suffering from internal bleeding, the once commanding and seemingly infallible supreme leader of the revolution was admitted to a hospital in May 1989 and died less than two weeks later on June 3.

Despite the harsh repressiveness of his regime, millions of Iranians poured into the streets nationwide, expressing genuine shock and grief. The first attempt at a funeral procession had to be canceled when his wooden casket was mobbed and nearly overturned and torn apart by mourners. The body itself almost fell to the ground as spectators grabbed for the burial shroud wrapped around Khomeini. The second funeral procession featured heavily armed security and a steel casket.

THE NEXT SUPREME LEADER

Clearly, the reverence and awe that many Iranians felt for Khomeini from his earliest days as a radical cleric 30 years before had remained largely undiminished. Khomeini was the father of the post-revolution Republic of Iran, and he would not be easily replaced. Whoever followed him as supreme leader would have enormous shoes to fill and would almost certainly suffer in comparison with Khomeini and not command the same respect, affection, and admiration.

Given the popular outpouring of grief and love, and the hard-line clerics' continued tight hold over Iranian society, the next supreme leader would feel pressure to hew closely to Ayatollah Khomeini's radical Islamic agenda and conservative social principles. The next supreme leader had no apparent mandate—certainly not from the Council of Guardians or Assembly of Experts—to seek political or social change or loosen the tight bonds between religion, government, and society.

Furthermore, lacking the charisma and command of Ayatollah Khomeini, the next supreme leader would not enjoy his predecessor's aura of infallibility. Whoever was chosen to replace Khomeini would occupy a very different position of leadership. He would have to share power with and mediate between the often liberal-leaning parliamentarians in the Majlis and the Iranian citizens they represented (who would no longer be cowed by Khomeini and many of whom were beginning to agitate for greater freedoms) and the conservative fundamentalist Council of Guardians. He would be supreme leader, but one who had to listen to the opinions of various political factions and respect the influence and authority of other branches of Iranian government. The days of the ayatollah's absolute power were over.

8
Supreme Leader Ayatollah Ali Khamenei

THE MAN WHO WOULD BECOME THE NEXT SUPREME LEADER OF IRAN and replace the venerable Ayatollah Khomeini was, to many observers, a surprising choice. On June 5, 1989, only two days after Khomeini's death, the Assembly of Experts selected Ali Khamenei to fill the position. Yet he had not originally been Khomeini's first choice as his heir to power.

For much of the previous decade, it was widely assumed that Khomeini's successor would be Ayatollah Hussein Ali Montazeri, a once radically fundamentalist cleric who had developed more liberal and outspoken opinions in recent years. While still a foreign policy hard-liner, with the "correct" anti-American and anti-Israel attitudes, he had become a forceful advocate for greater liberalization at home. He spoke out publicly in favor of greater freedom of the press and more humane treatment of political prisoners. In a letter

Khomeini is said to have expressed his wishes, while on his deathbed, that Ali Khamenei be chosen as his replacement.

to Khomeini, he declared that the ayatollah's intelligence and security agencies and the nation's prisons were worse than those in the darkest days of the shah and SAVAK. He claimed that Iran was becoming known worldwide primarily for its politically motivated executions. Needless to say, Montazeri fell out of favor with Khomeini and the conservative ruling clerics.

With the heir apparent on the outs, Khomeini is said to have expressed his wishes, while on his deathbed, that Ali Khamenei be chosen as his replacement. This endorsement was reported by Khomeini's son, Ahmad, and the cleric Ali Akbar Hashemi Rafsanjani (who would go on to become president of the republic), both men having spoken to Khomeini privately in the hours before his death. Even with Ayatollah Khomeini's apparent endorsement, however, selecting Ali Khamenei would not be an easy process.

DOUBTS ABOUT ALI KHAMENEI

Many of the clerics on the Assembly of Experts were uncomfortable with Khamenei's theological qualifications and accomplishments. His clerical education had been interrupted when he left Qom to care for his father, and his revolutionary activities of the mid-1960s and 1970s further prevented his studies. He remained a relatively low-ranking cleric, a hojjat-ol Islam. He had not yet been acclaimed by his fellow clerics as an ayatollah, much less an ayatollah al-uzma, a grand ayatollah, or a marja-e taqlid, a "source of emulation." As the Iranian Constitution was formulated at the time of Khomeini's death, the supreme leader was supposed to have been a grand ayatollah and a marja-e taqlid.

In addition, some of the clerics, realizing that no one would command the respect and absolute authority that Khomeini had enjoyed, believed that a council of conservative clerics should serve in the supreme leader's place. Ultimately, however, most of the assembly recognized that because Ali Khamenei didn't have much of a popular following and was a weak candidate who needed their support to attain a position of power, they were being presented with a valuable opportunity. They felt he could be easily controlled and influenced. Through him, they could exert far more power than they did under Khomeini, who was so strong and authoritative that he didn't need their backing in the way Ali Khamenei would.

The Assembly of Experts made their peace with the selection of Ali Khamenei as supreme leader. Much remained to be done, however, to make the appointment legitimate. Forty-two changes had to be made to the constitution to lower the religious requirements for the position. In addition, the assembly hastily conferred him with the title of ayatollah, though they opted not to grant him the honor of grand ayatollah. Interestingly, the religious establishment at Qom, where Ali Khamenei spent six years studying under Khomeini and other leading senior clerics, refuses to accept Khamenei's status as an ayatollah to this day. Several years later, they also rejected his proposed elevation to the status of marja-e taqlid for Shiites in Iran; in a compromise, however, he was allowed to serve as a marja to Shiites living outside of Iran.

Ali Khamenei was fully aware of the assembly's deliberations and his fellow clerics' reservations about his theological credentials. He understood that he was viewed by his peers as something of a lightweight—a cleric whose theological writings and academic achievements were elementary and lackluster and who was honored with the title ayatollah in haste and for the sake of political convenience. Many observers believe

KHAMEINI UNDERSTOOD THAT HE WAS VIEWED BY HIS PEERS AS A CLERIC WHO WAS HONORED WITH THE TITLE AYATOLLAH IN HASTE AND FOR THE SAKE OF POLITICAL CONVENIENCE.

this led to great insecurity in Ali Khamenei, prompting him to align himself more strictly with the fundamentalist senior clerics in an attempt to gain their favor and respect. These radical clerics dominated the Council of Guardians, the Assembly of Experts, and the judiciary, and commanded the loyalty of the armed forces, so if Ayatollah Khamenei hoped to wield any power as supreme leader, he needed to align himself with the conservative clergy.

RAFSANJANI'S ATTEMPTS AT REFORM

Ayatollah Khamenei's swing back towards conservatism following his relatively moderate period as president is illustrated by his changing relationship with his former ally and policy partner, Ali Akbar Hashemi Rafsanjani.

Formerly the speaker of the Majlis, Rafsanjani was now filling Ali Khamenei's old office as president. Initially, they continued their partnership, as Rafsanjani, with Ayatollah Khamenei's blessing, attempted to reform the nation's stagnating economy. Years of revolution, war, international sanctions, foreign debt, lowering oil prices, and mismanagement by clerics untrained in economics had left the economy in dire shape.

Rafsanjani surrounded himself with cabinet members and advisers who were educated in European and American universities, and he urged Iranian professionals and businesspeople who had left Iran during the reign of Khomeini to return home and lend their expertise, resources, and investment dollars to the struggling republic. He also undercut Khomeini's

As the new president of the republic, Ali Akbar Hashemi Rafsanjani took a more liberal approach. He allowed certain Western music, movies, and beauty products to be sold in Iran. In addition, the strict Islamic dress code was loosened in larger cities like Tehran. In the photograph above, Iranian women walk down the street wearing Western-style coats and bags.

longstanding insistence on placing social justice and the public welfare over sound financial planning by reducing or eliminating subsidies (artificially reduced prices) on such basics as milk, bread, meat, sugar, water, tea, and electricity. These were all courses of action that would have been unthinkable in the Khomeini years.

This liberalizing and "Westernizing" of the Iranian economy angered many conservative clerics in the Council of Guardians, yet what really stirred them up was Rafsanjani's attempts to loosen Khomeini's social restrictions. Sensing that the post-revolution and post-war generation of young people was getting impatient with limited freedom and the clerics' perpetual calls for sacrifice and discipline in service of the revolution, Rafsanjani hoped to avoid unrest among youths and students by granting them some small liberties. Popular—and, more important, secular—music was sold in record stores, certain American films were screened, and women's beauty products became more readily available. Even Islamic dress codes were unofficially relaxed in big cities like Tehran.

KHAMENEI'S SWING TO THE RIGHT

While he was willing to allow Rafsanjani some leeway in tackling Iran's economic problems, Ayatollah Khamenei felt the pressure of conservative clerics to stamp out the president's social reforms. He began to turn on his former ally Rafsanjani, a man who argued strenuously in favor of Khamenei's elevation to the position of supreme leader.

As conservative outrage over Rafsanjani's policies began to build, Ayatollah Khamenei weighed in and characterized the president and his fellow reformers as anti-Islamic, placing economic considerations over both love of God and love of humanity: "Some mock religious virtues, but if we spend billions on development projects and ignore moral issues, all achievements amount to nothing" (as quoted in Takeyh's *Hidden Iran*). With Ayatollah Khamenei's blessing, the police harassed and arrested anyone deemed to be violating the strict codes of Islamic behavior first imposed by Khomeini.

While currying favor with conservative clerics on the Council of Guardians by undercutting the authority of President Rafsanjani, Ayatollah Khamenei also set about to strengthen his position among these clerics and consolidate his power. He encouraged the Council of Guardians to reject almost one-third of the 169 candidates up for election to the Assembly of Experts. Officially, the candidates were rejected because of some questionable behavior in their past, a lack of experience with Islamic jurisprudence, or their refusal to take a theological test demanded by Khamenei. Because the Assembly of Experts was empowered to supervise, guide, and even remove the supreme leader, it was important to Ayatollah Khamenei to stock the assembly with allies—clerics who would not oppose or antagonize him or seek to undercut his authority. He also directed the Council of Guardians to disqualify any candidates for the Majlis with whom he disagreed, particularly liberal reformers and socialists. Thus, conservatives soon gained a majority in the Majlis, typically a more liberal-leaning Iranian government institution.

THE LIBERALIZATION MOVEMENT STALLS

While Ayatollah Khamenei was strengthening his support among the conservative clergy and gaining greater control over the Assembly of Experts and Majlis, President Rafsanjani was facing reelection. With his liberalization initiatives stalled and blocked by Khamenei and the economy continuing to falter, many Iranians felt disappointed with the man who seemed to offer so much hope for better, freer times back in 1989. Rafsanjani won reelection, but by a much smaller margin than in his first campaign. His diminished popularity among average Iranians strengthened Ayatollah Khamenei's hand and encouraged him to continue his more conservative drift. He did not have to worry that Rafsanjani had "people power" on his side.

Rafsanjani's second term would do nothing to reverse his political fortunes. The economy continued to stagnate, and the reduction and elimination of subsidies had led to increased prices for basic necessities, consumer goods, and services. Unemployment, especially among Iranian youths, was high, hovering around 30 percent. Social restrictions were as tight and repressive as ever. Despair and anger began to percolate on the streets, which were the scene of riots in 1994 and 1995.

Sensing that Rafsanjani was gravely wounded politically, Ayatollah Khamenei supported a group of conservative representatives in the Majlis in their attempts to block Rafsanjani's moderate economic, social, and foreign policy initiatives. As supreme leader, he used his veto power over Majlis legislation when necessary. Just as Khamenei had found years earlier, Rafsanjani discovered that the office of the president was not nearly powerful enough to do battle with the entrenched religious and business interests and effect a true reform of Iranian society.

A NEW REFORMER EMERGES

Though the Iranian populace had grown disenchanted with Rafsanjani and his reform efforts, this did not mean that their allegiances lay with Ayatollah Khamenei and the fundamentalist clergy and politicians. Indeed, as the next presidential election cycle approached in 1997, much popular support began to center upon a reformist intellectual and cleric named Muhammad Khatami.

Khatami's father had been one of Ayatollah Khamenei's favorite teachers at Mashhad, and the supreme leader had remained friends with him and his family. Under Rafsanjani, Muhammad Khatami had served as the minister of culture and Islamic guidance. He was forced out by conservative forces after granting licenses for publications and plays that contained material deemed to be in violation of the theocratic regime's moral and spiritual standards.

After being dismissed, Khatami supplemented his Islamic theology studies with classes in Western philosophy and began to advocate pro-democracy views. He once wrote that "state authority cannot be attained through coercion and dictatorship. Rather it is to be realized through governing according

Presidential candidate Muhammad Khatami greets his supporters outside of a polling station on election day in 1997. Khatami won the election and became Iran's fifth president. As the supreme leader, Ayatollah Khamenei confirmed his election.

to law, respecting the rights and empowering the people to participate and ensuring their involvement in decision making" (as quoted by Takeyh). Khatami further argued that, in order to hold the loyalties of young Iranians and reenergize the nation, Islam must adapt to the modern age. This surprisingly bold and direct challenge to—and critique of—Iran's theocracy caught the attention and won the hearts of many frustrated Iranians.

Claiming descent from the Prophet Muhammad and enjoying a long-term friendship with Ahmad Khomeini, the former supreme leader's son, Khatami seemed well-positioned to be able to succeed where Rafsanjani failed. His Islamic and revolutionary credentials were rock solid, seeming to provide him with some leverage against the obstructing conservative clerics in the Majlis and Council of Guardians. He began to enjoy much popular support, and many Iranians came to believe he was the best chance for reform, freedom, and a more open society. He won the 1997 presidential election in a landslide, and, as required by the constitution, Ayatollah Khamenei confirmed his election.

"DIALOGUE AMONG CIVILIZATIONS"

Khatami had run on a platform of change and reform. He promised to reduce the tyrannical rule of the clerics, respect civil liberties, and enlarge personal freedoms. He wished to establish a governing culture that was less defined and motivated by religious superstition and fanaticism. He intended to increase freedom of the press, decriminalize free expression and dissent, and nourish less restricted and censored cultural and artistic expression. Even more shocking and exciting to many Iranians, who had long endured the social repression and national isolation imposed by the ruling clerics, President Khatami wished to rejoin the community of nations and foster friendly and productive relations, even with former archenemies, including the United States.

Though this last policy direction alarmed and enraged the Khomeini-era clerics and the military—who still felt locked in a to-the-death ideological battle with America—it appealed to ordinary Iranians who had become disenchanted enough with Iran's theocracy to begin viewing it—not the "Great Satan" United States—as the enemy. Iranians, particularly the nation's young citizens, craved greater freedom, prosperity, and access to Western cultural and consumer goods. The

United States seemed to embody and offer all of these things so desperately desired.

Echoing Rafsanjani's foreign policy initiative when he was prime minister, Khatami put forth a proposal for a "dialogue among civilizations." Any nation could become a friend and partner with Iran, he argued, if it respected Iran's sovereignty and had no intention of meddling in its internal affairs or treating it with aggression. Similarly, Iran would vow not to meddle in other nation's affairs, particularly those of its Muslim neighbors, but instead it would seek change and find consensus through diplomacy and persuasion. Bullets and bombs would not be a part of Iran's foreign policy, if Khatami had his way. Mutual respect was the only real prerequisite for friendship.

The new president even went so far as to praise the American people and suggest a discussion and an exchange of ideas between the people of both nations. Yet, no doubt sensing he was courting the wrath of Ayatollah Khamenei and the ruling clerics, Khatami also insisted that the United States was entirely responsible for poor relations with Iran and its attitude must change before the relationship could improve. In addition, he singled out Israel as the one nation in the world with whom Iran would never have good relations.

This boldness followed by caution and partial retreat would characterize Khatami's reform efforts. Though he introduced startling new ideas and debates into the Iranian political scene, actual social and foreign policy progress would remain small. In the early days of the so-called "Tehran Spring"—a brief period of greater social and political freedoms—new publications that were often critical of the theocracy were allowed, and they operated with fewer censorship restrictions. Permits were readily granted for the formation of reform groups and the staging of political gatherings. Iran even mended fences with Saudi Arabia and the European Union, two longtime adversaries. These gains would prove to be short-lived, however. Conservative forces were aligning against Khatami and his Tehran Spring.

KHAMENEI'S STIFLING OF THE REFORM MOVEMENT

Ayatollah Khamenei and the ruling clerics, seeing how the people were so enthusiastically responding to Khatami's ideas and policies, genuinely feared that a popular movement might form around the president and lead to their overthrow. They quickly swung into action, first with stern words of warning and condemnation, then with a crackdown. Ayatollah Khamenei warned all Iranians that "the enemy is striking Islam at home" (as quoted by Takeyh) and that those who were seeking improved relations with the United States were "simpletons and traitors" (as quoted by Elaine Sciolino in her book *Persian Mirrors*).

Khamenei also urged his fellow clerics and officials under his control to sound ominous notes of warning as well. The commander of the Revolutionary Guards vowed to defend the revolution against "conspirators," claiming he was operating under the direct orders, and with the full support of, Ayatollah Khamenei. Other clerics claimed that Khatami and his fellow reformers were weakening the nation's Islamic institutions, spreading strife and disagreement among the people, and traitorously inviting American influence and control over Iran.

The clerics—and with them the military, the bonyads, the Council of Experts, the state press, and the judiciary—closed ranks and effectively stifled the reform movement. Using the judiciary and security services, Ayatollah Khamenei and the hard-liners shut down newspapers and other media outlets, imprisoned key reform leaders on trumped-up charges, and, through the Council of Guardians, vetoed reformist legislation and disqualified their political candidates from elections. This concerted effort at repression, coupled with the continuing woes of the Iranian economy and Khatami's timid, nonconfrontational approach to enacting reform measures, made many Iranians lose faith in the possibility of ever overcoming the theocracy's tight control over society. They also lost faith in Khatami.

Iranian students try to hide their faces from tear gas bombs as demonstrations erupt between student supporters of liberal-minded Muhammad Khatami and conservative Islamic militiamen. Khatami had a large student following due to his allowance of personal freedoms and civil liberties. Ayatollah Khamenei and his conservative followers feared Khatami's strong student following and cracked down on Khatami's reform movements, causing demonstrations and riots.

The final straw came in 1999 and 2000 when new restrictions on the press were instituted and enforced, prompted by a wave of newspaper stories featuring frank critiques of the theocracy, exposing the regime's corruption and political violence, and calling into question the wisdom and legitimacy of religious rule. Numerous newspaper offices were shut around the country, including Tehran University's student newspaper. This closure led to campus protests that quickly spread to other cities and ignited large anti-regime demonstrations and riots.

IT BECAME CLEAR THAT KHATAMI HAD BEEN NEUTRALIZED BY AYATOLLAH KHAMENEI AND THE RULING ELITE.

The students looked to Khatami for support and hoped this might be the spark of a new revolution, or at the very least a decisive shift of power toward the reformists. Yet Khatami, ever cautious and wary of taking on Ayatollah Khamenei and the radical clerics head-on, refused to align himself with the free-press rioters. Instead, he pleaded with them to halt their demonstrations, then ultimately joined Khamenei in condemning the riots.

At this point, it became clear that Khatami had been neutralized by Ayatollah Khamenei and the ruling elite. He easily won reelection in 2001, but the turnout was lower than in 1997, and he and his followers seemed to have been broken in spirit. When announcing his candidacy for reelection, he tearfully admitted, "Personally, I'd prefer to be somewhere else" (as quoted in Sciolino's *Persian Mirrors*). Following his reelection, he acknowledged that he just didn't have enough power to provide Iranians with the freedoms they were entitled to under the constitution. Like Rafsanjani and Ali Khamenei before him, Khatami had run up against the limitations of his office and the nearly absolute control of the theocracy now led by Ayatollah Khamenei, the former president who had crossed over to the shadowy source of power occupied by the Khomeini-era radical clerics.

MANAGING IRANIAN FRUSTRATION AND ANGER

Though Ayatollah Khamenei had effectively sidelined President Khatami and the reformists, he did recognize the vein of anger, restlessness, and frustration among Iran's youth that Khatami had tapped into. Realizing that such unrest could kindle and burst into a new Iranian revolution that would sweep him and his fellow conservative clerics out of power—like the shah before him and in a modern version of a Zoroastrian-era removal of an evil king—Ayatollah Khamenei decided to sacrifice some of his hard-line Islamic ideals and offer Iranians limited freedoms in order to preserve his hold on power.

Against a backdrop of occasional widespread student protests in 2002 and 2003 and ongoing high unemployment rates, Khamenei and the Council of Guardians agreed to relax some social controls. Women began to wear makeup and jewelry, shorter veils, and more form-fitting coats and trousers. Public displays of affection between couples were no longer punished. Parties were not raided and shut down by the police, and satellite dishes—an important link to the Western world and its alternate perspectives and dissenting opinions—began to proliferate.

Even the supreme leader tried to soften his image. News stories were carefully planted describing his enthusiasm for soccer and his love of poetry and music. It was hoped that if young Iranians could be distracted and appeased with minor new social freedoms, the dangerous energy of their political anger would dissipate and allow the regime to continue on as always, with its power undiminished.

TAMPERING WITH ELECTIONS

Not trusting only this strategy of trading limited social liberty for political stability, the Council of Guardians, with Ayatollah Khamenei's blessing, prepared for the 2004 general election by disqualifying nearly a third of the candidates (2,500 of the 8,000 applying to run for seats), the vast majority of them reformists. By stacking the election against the reformists, the council was hoping to end up with a Majlis that was dominated by conservatives, thereby further consolidating their power and strengthening their already tight grip on Iranian government, culture, and society.

Reformists cried foul but did not have enough leverage—and no real power—to be able to do anything about it. Having lost the trust of Iranian youth, who felt betrayed by the reformists' weak-kneed stance before the regime, especially during the press freedom riots, Khatami's faction could no longer even count on people power.

The Council of Guardians' tampering with the election was outrageous enough to prompt some opposition clerics to speak up and condemn the regime in unusually blunt terms. Ayatollah Khomeini's one-time heir apparent and designated successor, Ayatollah Hussein Ali Montazeri, dismissed the legitimacy of the upcoming elections. Despite having been recently released from a five-year period of house arrest, imposed by Khamenei after Montazeri called the supreme leader "incompetent," the liberal cleric declared, "Elections in these circumstances will be of no use, and they will not be free. . . . Even I, who used to be a leading figure in the revolution, have not the right to speak out. Authoritarianism will never last long. The gentlemen in power must submit to the wishes of the people, or they will be swept away" (as quoted in a February 17, 2004, CNN.com article). Reformists called for a boycott of the elections. Only half of all eligible voters showed up at the polls, and the result was a solid conservative majority in the Majlis.

Ayatollah Montazeri's prediction of a popular uprising and regime change did not come to pass after the 2004 elections, but the ruling elite did not get exactly what they had hoped and planned for, either. A new challenge to their authority was about to be issued, and this time it would come from within their own ranks.

9

Khamenei and Iran's Future

AYATOLLAH KHAMENEI'S CHOICE FOR PRESIDENT HAD BEEN ALI LARIJANI, the son of a grand ayatollah who received an education at some of the leading religious centers in Iran and was married to the daughter of a leading cleric. Despite his studies of Western philosophy and his introduction of sports and entertainment programming to television when he headed the state broadcasting organization, he was said to be a hard-liner and a "true believer" in Khomeini's revolution.

Though Khamenei's choice, Larijani was not considered the front-runner. This position was held by Ali Akbar Hashemi Rafsanjani, the former Majlis speaker and president of the republic. Yet, because he was still primarily remembered by the Iranian people as the man who was unable to boost employment levels and instead slashed subsidies on basic goods, resulting in sharp price increases in the 1990s, he lost the election. A third man, who seemingly came out of nowhere, rode a tide of populist anger and enthusiasm to seize the office.

THE CANDIDATE OF THE POOR AND DISILLUSIONED

The new president of Iran was named Mahmoud Ahmadinejad. The former mayor of Tehran, Ahmadinejad was intent on reviving the revolutionary fervor of the Iranian population, especially Khomeini's commitment to social justice. He was less interested in discussing the social freedoms promoted by the reformists and more interested in vowing to wage war on poverty, unemployment, and corruption in politics and business.

With the reformists and their urban, educated, liberal political base boycotting the elections, Ahmadinejad managed to parlay his popularity with rural peasants and laborers and the urban poor into a shocking election victory. Because of his apparent commitment to social justice and economic fairness, many people believed him to be more pure in his Islamic faith than many of the old-guard clerics, who were increasingly viewed by the Iranian populace as corrupted by power, more interested in preserving their positions of influence than in serving God's will. Once again, the Zoroastrian notion of the righteous man being elevated over leaders who prove themselves to be corrupt and serving the interests of evil seemed to be reasserting itself.

Ayatollah Khamenei and the ruling clerics got some of what they wanted in the 2004 elections. They had broken the back of the reformists and gained a conservative majority in the Majlis. Their presidential candidate did not win, but they did end up with a man who was strongly conservative and still fired by Khomeini's revolutionary ideals. They could work with this man, they believed, but his ability to harness the enormous energy of people power would require close watching.

On August 6, 2005, Mahmoud Ahmadinejad became the sixth president of Iran. The former mayor of Tehran, Ahmadinejad has used his presidency to promote conservative ideals that have alienated much of the Western world. With his continuation of the Iranian nuclear program and his declaration that the Holocaust was a myth, Ahmadinejad remains a controversial figure.

A POPULIST FIREBRAND

Just how conservative President Ahmadinejad was would quickly become apparent. In 2005, he made several speeches stating that Israel should be "wiped off the map" (or "erased from the pages of history," depending on the translation). He expressed doubts about the historical reality of the Holocaust and convened a conference of well-known Holocaust deniers to discuss the issue and arrive at conclusions.

Though not attempting to roll back the minor social freedoms allowed by Ayatollah Khamenei before the elections, Ahmadinejad did replace many government officials with members of the intelligence and security services. As a result, politically motivated arrests of journalists, bloggers, and other opponents increased. Most dramatically, he aggressively took on the United States over the issue of Iran's right to develop its nuclear program. It is this provocation that has caused a widening split between the conservativism of the Council of Guardians and Ayatollah Khamenei and that of President Ahmadinejad.

IRAN'S NUCLEAR PROGRAM

Ayatollah Khamenei has said conflicting things about Iran's nuclear ambitions. Though he has repeatedly issued *fatwas* (religious rulings) condemning the production, stockpiling, and use of nuclear weapons, he has also insisted that Iran must maintain a strong army to be able to confront its enemies and all foreign aggressors. He has also vowed that the country will not back down from its right to develop nuclear technology, though he insisted the program was designed for peaceful purposes only.

Iran is a signer of the international nuclear nonproliferation treaty (an agreement designed to prevent the worldwide spread of nuclear technology and weaponry), and it has never been caught violating the agreement. Yet for almost 20 years it has kept some of its nuclear activities secret from International Atomic Energy Agency (IAEA) inspectors. Many Iranians believe that if Israel, Pakistan, and India can possess nuclear weapons, there is no reason Iran should not be able to. It is an issue of autonomy and nationalism more than a desire to be threatening. Many also believe nuclear weapons would be

IN AUGUST 2005, IRAN ANNOUNCED THAT IT HAD BEGUN CONVERTING URANIUM INTO A GAS THAT COULD BE FURTHER PURIFIED FOR USE IN WEAPONS AND THAT IT HAD REOPENED A URANIUM ENRICHMENT PLANT.

an invaluable deterrent against American aggression, invasion, or "regime change" of the sort witnessed in neighboring Iraq. Yet this nationalist and essentially defensive interest in nuclear technology took on a more ominous cast following President Ahmadinejad's anti-Israel and anti-Semitic rants, and his brazen taunting of the United States.

In August 2005, Iran announced that it had begun converting uranium into a gas that could be further purified for use in weapons and that it had reopened a uranium enrichment plant. This news threw the world, already anxious over North Korea's nuclear ambitions, into a near panic. An ongoing series of diplomatic efforts were launched to attempt to persuade, threaten, and punish Iran into complying with international law and drop any weapons programs it was developing. On December 23, 2006, the United Nations Security Council passed a resolution condemning Iran's uranium enrichment program and imposing a ban on the trade of goods related to the program. It gave Iran two months to halt the program or be faced with harsher and more wide-ranging sanctions.

The nuclear stalemate continued, with the United States claiming Iran was building nuclear weapons and Iran insisting the nuclear program is merely designed to generate electricity. As of July 2007, Iran continued to ignore UN demands to suspend its nuclear fuel activity. Two sets of UN sanctions were passed against Iran, with a third set being prepared.

Iran's nuclear program has been a cause of contention between Iranians and the Western world. Due to the Iranian president's anti-United States and anti-Semitic remarks, many fear that Iran would stockpile nuclear weapons to use as forms of mass destruction. In the photograph above, missiles are seen in front of a photograph of Iran's supreme leader at a 2005 war exhibit.

AHMADINEJAD AND A NEW PERSIAN EMPIRE

Much of this crisis atmosphere was created by Ahmadinejad's fiery speeches, promising the inevitability of a nuclear-armed Iran and daring the United States and Europe to do something to try to stop it. His anti-Israel, anti-United States rants played well with many Muslims throughout the Islamic world, and it is believed Ahmadinejad hopes to extend his power through his fiery rhetoric. In doing so, he hopes to place Iran at the pinnacle of the Islamic world—its political and cultural leader—and at the vanguard of the East-West ideological conflict. In his outward-looking, confrontational version of Islamic militancy, he seems to wish to achieve a new Persian Empire—a sweeping, powerful, dominating sphere of influence centered in, built upon, and controlled by Iran. The first step in this process of creating a "Greater Iran" may be a strengthening of ties with Iraq's Shiite majority, a development that has the United States gravely concerned.

The conservative Khomeini-era clerics, including Ayatollah Khamenei, seem to favor a far less confrontational brand of Islamic militancy. They have grown inward-looking, comfortable in their isolation from the world, and relatively free of its interference and meddling. While Ahmadinejad harkens back to the expansive glories of the Persian Empire, its acquisition of far-reaching territory and influence, the conservative clerics value the former empire's impregnability, its security from invasion and conquest. In the wake of years of international meddling and exploitation, the Islamic revolution, the Iran-Iraq War, ongoing American hostility, and threats of pro-Western secularization, the former revolutionaries have developed a siege mentality. At this point, they seem more interested in developing a Fortress Islam than a holy war.

Yet Ayatollah Khamenei continues to send mixed signals to the United States and baffle Western political observers. Responding to Washington's claims that Iran is encouraging sectarian violence in Iraq by funding and arming Iraqi Shiites, Khamenei agreed to three-way security talks with United States and Iraqi representatives in Baghdad in July 2007, the first official diplomatic exchange between Iran and the United States since ties were severed after the 1979 Iranian Revolution and ensuing hostage crisis. Yet only days after this dramatic warming of relations, Khamenei again dampened expectations and dashed hopes for reconciliation and renewed cooperation by declaring the United States and Israel to be Iran's chief enemies.

ALI KHAMENEI AGAIN CLOSES RANKS

Sensing a split developing in the conservative ranks between the old-guard clerics and the populist and nationalist firebrands led by Ahmadinejad, Ayatollah Khamenei acted to curb the president's growing influence, just as he had earlier marginalized Rafsanjani and Khatami. He appointed Ali Larijani to serve as head of the National Security Council and as Iran's chief nuclear negotiator, thereby hoping to keep Ahmadinejad out of the nuclear debate. Though also insisting on Iran's right to a uranium enrichment program, Larijani prefers to foster Iran's nuclear capabilities while forging amicable relationships with the world powers. Diplomacy and courtesy, not provocation, are his methods.

Ayatollah Khamenei further tried to neutralize and marginalize the president by ordering the creation of a foreign policy council—the Strategic Council for Foreign Relations—that would answer only to him and would bypass Ahmadinejad altogether. Ayatollah Khamenei would have to proceed carefully, however, because Ahmadinejad appeared to enjoy the support and enthusiasm of Iran's armed forces, a powerful and influential player within the Iranian power structure.

Hoping to provide a moderate counterbalance to Ahmadinejad's hard-line and potentially dangerous and destabilizing belligerence, Ayatollah Khamenei urged Ali Akbar Hashemi Rafsanjani to run for the Assembly of Experts in December 2006. Rafsanjani trounced his opponent, an ultraconservative aligned with Ahmadinejad. Though once squeezed out of power by Khamenei for being too moderate, Rafsanjani's pragmatism was now invaluable to the supreme leader, who sensed the grave threat of Ahmadinejad's reckless Islamist populism.

With Iranian politics and population constantly changing, Ayatollah Ali Khamanei remains a strong leader for his country. But as Iran and the rest of the world stand on the brink of change, the supreme leader's future is similarly uncertain.

Following the Majlis' decision in January 2007, prompted by Ahmadinejad, to bar IAEA inspectors from entering Iran, two state-controlled newspapers (one owned by Ayatollah Khamenei) condemned the president's actions and called on him to stay out of the nuclear debate. The conservative clerics found an unlikely ally in the outspoken opposition leader Ayatollah Montazeri (who had long criticized Khamenei and had been placed under house arrest by him). "One has to deal with the enemy with wisdom. We should not provoke the enemy," he warned, "otherwise the country will be faced with problems" (as quoted in a January 23, 2007, *New York Times* article).

AHMADINEJAD'S INFLUENCE WEAKENS

Once again, the revolutionary-era ruling elite, guided by Ayatollah Khamenei, had closed ranks, this time joined by their usual opponents—the moderates and reformists—to halt the progress of a president whose policies and popularity threatened the entrenched power structure. Once again, the effort seemed to have worked.

In the December 2006 elections for Iran's city councils and the Assembly of Experts, President Ahmadinejad's candidates were soundly defeated, while reformists and Khamenei-aligned conservatives gained ground. In mid-January, faced with persistent unemployment and inflation—the longtime woes of the Iranian economy—more than half of the members of the Majlis, including many of Ahmadinejad's former allies, signed a letter criticizing the failure of his economic policies.

In 2007, popular dissatisfaction with Ahmadinejad's failing policies and broken promises resulted in widespread salary protests, strikes, and riots over rationing of gas and the resulting increase in prices for basic goods. In June 2007, a group of 57 economists publicly blasted the president for ignoring basic economic principles. They warned that government

NUCLEAR WEAPONS TECHNOLOGY SEEMS TO BE WITHIN IRAN'S GRASP, BUT SO TOO DO IMPROVED RELATIONS WITH BOTH ISLAMIC NEIGHBORS AND WESTERN NATIONS.

mismanagement was inflicting massive damage to the economy and that an economic crisis was imminent.

Promises of economic justice are what swept Ahmadinejad into power, and the election results and growing parliamentary opposition seemed to signal that his popularity was waning. He had delivered provocation and international outrage and trade penalties, but not jobs. Indeed, his stirring up of the international community may have invited the kind of foreign meddling and intrusiveness that Iran has long loathed and the economic sanctions it can ill afford.

AYATOLLAH ALI KHAMENEI AND THE PATH TO IRAN'S FUTURE

Ayatollah Khamenei appears to have once again skillfully consolidated his power and deftly managed Iran's perpetual competing currents of reform and religion, change and tradition, unrest and repression. He and all of Iran stand at the brink of a momentous turning point.

The revolutionary-era clerics are aging and increasingly challenged by reformists and younger conservatives advocating a more aggressive form of Islamic fundamentalism, one that seeks to spread beyond Iran's borders and engage and influence the world beyond. Nuclear weapons technology seems to be within Iran's grasp, but so too do improved relations both with Islamic neighbors—including Iraq with its Shiite majority—and Western nations. A moderation of Islamist revolutionary ideals could lead to greater prosperity and global involvement, while a retreat into hard-line conservatism could further Iran's isolation and economic strain. Continued repressive theocratic rule could continue to benefit the clerical and business elite while alienating the populace, or an increased trust in the processes of democracy could revitalize the nation and lead to a cultural flourishing unrivaled since the height of the Persian Empire.

What direction Khamenei chooses to take in leading Iran forward will largely determine whether Iran remains Fortress Islam or establishes a new Persian Empire across the Muslim world and beyond. It will define his legacy as well, and determine whether he retains the support of the people. If enough of the Iranian people ever deem him to be serving the forces of evil rather than good, if they conclude that he is not serving the best interests of the people and the nation but is only satisfying his own hunger for power, one way or another, they will reject his rule. They will shift their allegiances to another leader, a modern-day king of kings, who obeys God's will and provides justice to his people. For thousands of years Iranians have passed judgment on their leaders—even the most absolute and tyrannical of leaders—and occasionally have mustered the will and numbers to oust them. If Ayatollah Khamenei neglects to respect his people's power and pay heed to their desires, they could very well do so again.

CHRONOLOGY

1939 Ali Khamenei is born in Mashhad, Iran.

1943 Ali Khamenei begins attending a maktab, an Islamic
elementary school. He goes on to high school and the
Sulayman Khan Madrassa, a theological seminary
in Mashhad.

1952 The radical cleric Sayyed Mujtaba Nawwab Safawi
visits the madrassa and inspires anti-shah sentiments
in Ali Khamenei.

1957 Ali Khamenei finishes intermediate studies and begins
classes in the highest level of Islamic jurisprudence. He
travels to Najaf, Iraq, on pilgrimage and stays there for
a year to continue his studies.

1958 At the urging of his father, Ali Khamenei returns to
Iran and resumes his studies at the renowned seminary
in the holy city of Qom. It is here that he meets and
studies under Ayatollah Khomeini.

1962 Ali Khamenei joins Ayatollah Khomeini's
revolutionary movement.

1964–1977 Ali Khamenei spreads Ayatollah Khomeini's message of
anti-shah revolution throughout Iran via his writings,
speeches, and sermons. He is repeatedly arrested,
imprisoned, mistreated, and tortured by agents of
the SAVAK, the shah's secret police force. Ayatollah
Khomeini lives in exile in Najaf, Iraq, and Paris, France.

1977–1978 Ali Khamenei is sent into exile to Iranshahr in
southeastern Iran.

1979 Ali Khamenei ends his exile and cofounds the Islamic
Republic Party. The shah flees Iran. Ayatollah Khomeini

returns from exile in Paris and soon seizes control of Iran's provisional government, imposes sharia law, and establishes himself as supreme leader.

1979–1980 Khamenei becomes secretary of defense; supervisor of the Revolutionary Guards; leader of Tehran's Friday congregational prayers; and the Tehran representative in the Majlis.

1979–1981 Sixty-three American hostages are held in the U.S. embassy in Tehran by radical Iranian university students for 444 days. The students' actions were publicly supported by both Ayatollah Khomeini and Ali Khamenei.

1981 Ayatollah Khomeini appoints Ali Khamenei as his representative to the Supreme Defense Council. He is also appointed the chairman of the Cultural Revolution Council. Ali Khamenei survives an assassination attempt that permanently damages his arm, vocal chords, and lungs. He is elected to the presidency of the Republic of Iran.

1985 Ali Khamenei is reelected to the presidency.

1987 Ali Khamenei is named president of the Expediency Council.

1989 Ayatollah Khomeini dies. Ali Khamenei is given the title ayatollah and is chosen by the Assembly of Experts to be Iran's supreme leader. Ali Khamenei also serves as chairman of the Committee for the Revision of the Constitution. Ali Akbar Hashemi Rafsanjani is elected president of Iran.

1993 Rafsanjani is reelected as president.

1997 Muhammad Khatami is elected president of Iran and launches his "dialogue among civilizations" liberalizing policy initiatives.

1999–2000 Widespread student protests erupt over restrictive new press laws and the shutting down of opposition newspapers. President Khatami condemns the riots and supports the press restrictions.

2001 President Khatami is reelected.

2002–2003 Widespread student protests erupt again. Ayatollah Khamenei oversees a slight relaxing of strict Islamic codes of social behavior and dress codes.

2004 An ultraconservative populist named Mahmoud Ahmadinejad wins the presidency and promptly alarms the world with anti-Israel rants, taunts of the United States, boasts of Iran's nuclear program, and an aggressive foreign and nuclear policy.

2006 The United Nations Security Council imposes a trade embargo on goods exported to Iran that could be used in its uranium enrichment program and gives the nation two months to halt the program. Ahmadinejad's allies fare poorly in nationwide elections. Ayatollah Khamenei creates a national security council that answers only to him and does not involve President Ahmadinejad. Rafsanjani is elected to the Assembly of Experts.

2007 Iran refuses entry to International Atomic Energy Agency inspectors. President Ahmadinejad is reprimanded by several leading clerics for his aggressive foreign policy and his reckless involvement in Iran's nuclear negotiations. UN sanctions are passed against Iran for ignoring demands to halt its nuclear enrichment program. Ayatollah Khamenei agrees to joint U.S.-Iraqi-Iranian security talks in Baghdad. Days after a round of these talks, he declares the United States and Israel to be Iran's greatest enemies.

BIBLIOGRAPHY

"A Brief Biography of Ayatollah al-Udhma Sayyid Ali Khamenei," Islamic Centre, London. 1999. Available online. http://www.khamenei.de/biograph/biogricel.htm.

"A Brief Biography of the Life of His Eminence Ayatollah Khamenei, the Leader of the Islamic Republic in Iran," The Islamic Revolution Cultural-Research Institute for Preserving and Publishing Works by Ayatollah Seyyed Ali Khanenei. Available online. http://www.khamenei.ir/EN/Biography/index.jsp.

"Ayatollah Khamenei: Strong Military Needed to Deter Iran's Enemies," Voice of America. Available online. http://www.voanews.com/english/archive/2006-09/2006-09-20-voa35.cfm?CFID=91920586&CFTOKEN=53725437.

"Biography," The Office of the Supreme Leader Sayyid Ali Khamenei." Available online. http://www.leader.ir/langs/EN/index.php?p=bio.

"Biography of H.E. Ayatollah Sayyed Ali Khamenei: The Leader of the Islamic Republic of Iran," Salam Iran. Available online. http://www.salamiran.org/IranInfo/State/Leadership/Leader/LeaderBiography.html.

Clawson, Patrick, and Michael Rubin. *Eternal Iran: Continuity and Chaos.* New York: Palgrave Macmillan, 2005.

Fathi, Nazila. "Iran Bars Inspectors; Cleric Criticizes President." *New York Times.* January 23, 2007, p. A7.

Harper, Liz, "Governing Iran: Ayatollah Ali Khamenei," Online NewsHour. Available online. http://www.pbs.org/newshour/indepth_coverage/middle_east/iran/leader_khamenei.html.

Hiro, Dilip. *The Iranian Labyrinth: Journeys Through Theocratic Iran and Its Furies.* New York: Nation Books, 2005.

Keddie, Nikki R. *Modern Iran: Roots and Results of Revolution.* New Haven, Conn.: Yale University Press, 2006.

Mackey, Sandra. *The Iranians: Persia, Islam, and the Soul of a Nation.* New York: Plume, 1998.

Molavi, Afshin. *The Soul of Iran: A Nation's Journey to Freedom.* New York: W.W. Norton, 2002.

Naji, Kasra. "Reformists Criticize Iran's Supreme Leader on Elections," CNN.com. February 19, 2004. Available online. http://edition.cnn.com/2004/WORLD/meast/02/17/iran.elections/index.html.

Pollack, Kenneth M. *The Persian Puzzle: The Conflict Between Iran and America.* New York: Random House, 2004.

"Profile: Ayatollah Ali Khamenei," BBC News. Available online. http://news.bbc.co.uk/1/hi/world/middle_east/3018932.stm.

Reuters. "Iran's Khamenei Says No Retreat on Atomic Rights," Epoch Times. Available online. http://en.epochtimes.com/news/6-10-10/46870.html.

Ridgeon, Lloyd, ed. *Religion and Politics in Modern Iran: A Reader.* New York: I.B. Tauris, 2005.

Sciolino, Elaine. *Persian Mirrors: The Elusive Face of Iran.* New York: Touchstone, 2000.

Secor, Laura. "Whose Iran?" *New York Times.* January 28, 2007, section 6, p. 48.

Slackman, Michael. "A Cleric Steeped in Ways of Power," *New York Times.* September 9, 2006. Available online. http://travel2.nytimes.com/2006/09/09/world/middleeast/09khamenei.html.

Spindle, Bill. "In Iran, Two Power Centers Vie Amid Standoff Over Nuclear Fuel." *Wall Street Journal.* October 13, 2006, p. A1.

Taketh, Ray. *Hidden Iran: Paradox and Power in the Islamic Republic.* New York: Times Books, 2006.

United Press International. "Report: Khamenei Seeks to Regain Control," The Intelligence Summit. Available online. http://intelligence-summit.blogspot.com/2006/10/report-khamenei-seeks-to-regain.html.

Wright, Robin. *The Last Great Revolution: Turmoil and Transformation in Iran.* New York: Vintage Books, 2001.

Further Reading

Ansari, Ali. *A History of Modern Iran Since 1921: The Pahlavis and After.* New York: Longman, 2003.

Daniel, Elton L. *The History of Iran.* Westport, Conn.: Greenwood Press, 2000.

Ebadi, Shirin. *Iran Awakening: A Memoir of Revolution and Hope.* New York: Random House, 2005.

Egendorf, Laura K., ed. *Iran: Opposing Viewpoints.* Farmington Hills, Mich.: Greenhaven, 2006.

Encyclopedia Britannica. *Iran: The Essential Guide to a Country on the Brink.* Hoboken, N.J.: Wiley, 2006.

Esposito, John L., and R.K. Ramazani, eds. *Iran at the Crossroads.* New York: Palgrave Macmillan, 2000.

Gheissari, Ali, and Vali Nasr. *Democracy In Iran: History and the Quest for Liberty.* New York: Oxford University Press, 2006.

Kheirabadi, Masoud. *Iran.* New York: Chelsea House, 2003.

Kinzer, Stephen. *All the Shah's Men: An American Coup and the Roots of Middle East Terror.* Hoboken, N.J.: Wiley, August 2004.

Kurzman, Charles. *The Unthinkable Revolution in Iran.* Cambridge, Mass.: Harvard University Press, 2005.

Moin, Baqer. *Khomeini: Life of the Ayatollah.* New York: Thomas Dunne Books, 2000.

Ramen, Fred. *A Historical Atlas of Iran.* New York: The Rosen Publishing Group, 2003.

Satrapi, Marjane. *Persepolis: The Story of a Childhood.* New York: Pantheon, 2003.

Todd, Anne M., and Daniel E. Harmon. *Ayatollah Ruhollah Khomeini.* New York: Chelsea House, 2004.

Willett, Edward. *Ayatollah Khomeini.* New York: The Rosen Publishing Group, 2003.

PHOTO CREDITS

INDEX

About the Authors

JOHN MURPHY has a master's degree in medieval literature and is interested in the centuries-long interaction between the Western and Eastern worlds, a dialogue that has been by turns contentious and mutually enriching. He has written several books for young adults on history, politics, and government.

ARTHUR M. SCHLESINGER, JR. is remembered as the leading American historian of our time. He won the Pulitzer Prize for his books *The Age of Jackson* (1945) and *A Thousand Days* (1965), which also won the National Book Award. Professor Schlesinger was the Albert Schweitzer Professor of the Humanities at the City University of New York and was involved in several other Chelsea House projects, including the series *Revolutionary War Leaders*, *Colonial Leaders*, and *Your Government*.